# BLACKOUT POETRY JOURNAL

# Blackout Poetry

Blackout poetry is poetry created by rethinking existing text into something new and fresh. The fun comes in blacking out words you wish to eliminate and keeping those that create new art. This journal offers prompts and texts from some of the greatest writers in history to be altered and reinvented. There are no rules. Just be creative! Blackout, scribble and draw your way to inspiration.

## Styles of Blackouts

Classic

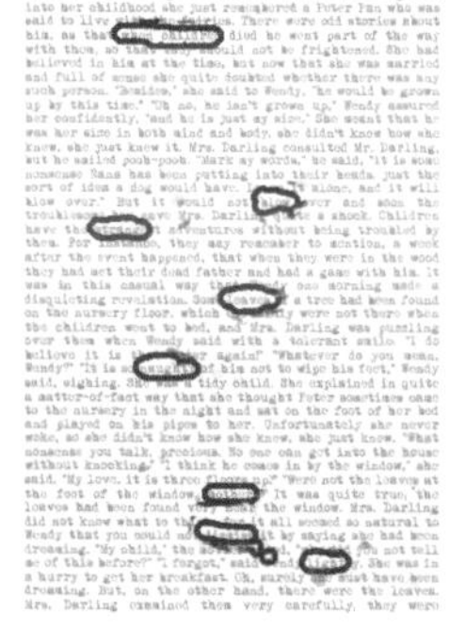

Circles

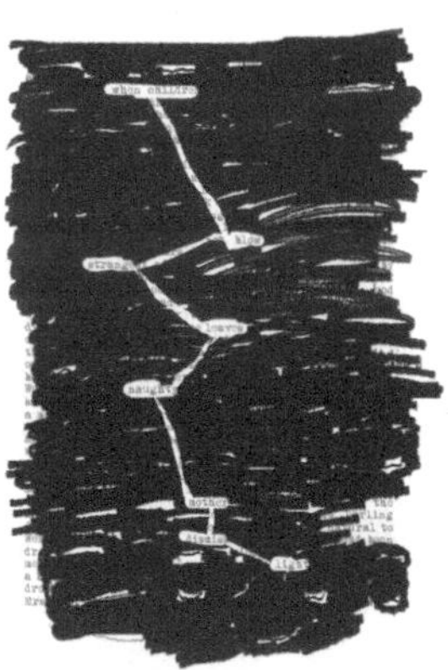

Plumbing

Multi-Colored

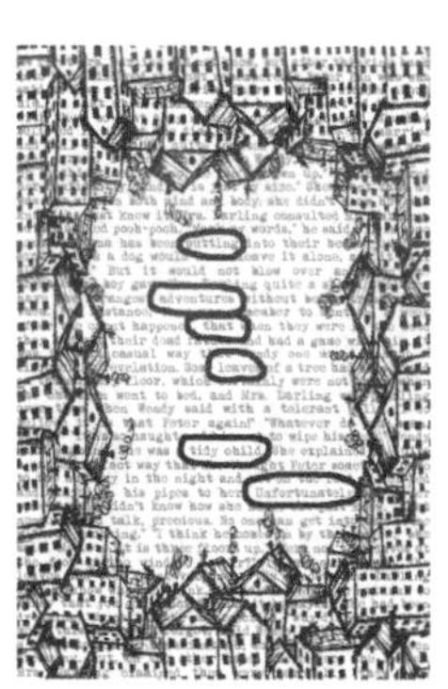

Doodles

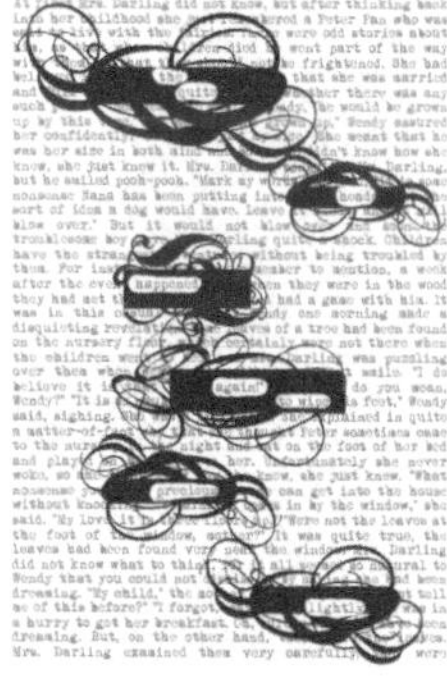

Swirls

# Create a poem about Love

"My love, it is three floors up." "Were not the leaves at the foot of the window, mother?" It was quite true; the leaves had been found very near the window. Mrs. Darling did not know what to think, for it all seemed so natural to Wendy that you could not dismiss it by saying she had been dreaming. "My child," the mother cried, "why did you not tell me of this before?" "I forgot," said Wendy lightly. She was in a hurry to get her breakfast. Oh, surely she must have been dreaming. But, on the other hand, there were the leaves. Mrs. Darling examined them very carefully; they were skeleton leaves, but she was sure they did not come from any tree that grew in England. She crawled about the floor, peering at it with a candle for marks of a strange foot. She rattled the poker up the chimney and tapped the walls. She let down a tape from the window to the pavement, and it was a sheer drop of thirty feet, without so much as a spout to climb up by. Certainly Wendy had been dreaming. But Wendy had not been dreaming, as the very next night showed, the night on which the extraordinary adventures of these children may be said to have begun. On the night we speak of all the children were once more in bed. It happened to be Nana's evening off, and Mrs. Darling had bathed them and sung to them till one by one they had let go her hand and slid away into the land of sleep. All were looking so safe and cosy that she smiled at her fears now and sat down tranquilly by the fire to sew. It was something for Michael, who on his birthday was getting into shirts. The fire was warm, however, and the nursery dimly lit by three night-lights, and presently the sewing lay on Mrs. Darling's lap. Then her head nodded, oh, so gracefully. She was asleep. Look at the four of them, Wendy and Michael over there, John here, and Mrs. Darling by the fire. There should have been a fourth night-light. While she slept she had a dream. She dreamt that the Neverland had come too near and that a strange boy had broken through from it. He did not alarm her, for she thought she had seen him before in the faces of many women who have no children. Perhaps he is to be found in the faces of some mothers also. But in her dream he had rent the film that obscures the Neverland, and she saw Wendy and John and Michael peeping through the gap.The dream by itself would have been a trifle, but while she was dreaming the window of the nursery blew open, and a boy did drop on the floor. He was accompanied by a strange light, no bigger than your fist, which darted about the room like a living thing and I think it must have been this light that

PETER PAN
BY J. M. BARRIE

# Create a poem about Childhood

It was horrible to think that I had provided the weapon, however undesignedly, but I could hardly think otherwise. I suffered unspeakable trouble while I considered and reconsidered whether I should at last dissolve that spell of my childhood and tell Joe all the story. For months afterwards, I every day settled the question finally in the negative, and reopened and reargued it next morning. The contention came, after all, to this;—the secret was such an old one now, had so grown into me and become a part of myself, that I could not tear it away. In addition to the dread that, having led up to so much mischief, it would be now more likely than ever to alienate Joe from me if he believed it, I had a further restraining dread that he would not believe it, but would assort it with the fabulous dogs and veal-cutlets as a monstrous invention. However, I temporized with myself, of course—for, was I not wavering between right and wrong, when the thing is always done?—and resolved to make a full disclosure if I should see any such new occasion as a new chance of helping in the discovery of the assailant. The Constables and the Bow Street men from London—for, this happened in the days of the extinct red-waistcoated police—were about the house for a week or two, and did pretty much what I have heard and read of like authorities doing in other such cases. They took up several obviously wrong people, and they ran their heads very hard against wrong ideas, and persisted in trying to fit the circumstances to the ideas, instead of trying to extract ideas from the circumstances. Also, they stood about the door of the Jolly Bargemen, with knowing and reserved looks that filled the whole neighborhood with admiration; and they had a mysterious manner of taking their drink, that was almost as good as taking the culprit. But not quite, for they never did it. Long after these constitutional powers had dispersed, my sister lay very ill in bed. Her sight was disturbed, so that she saw objects multiplied, and grasped at visionary teacups and wineglasses instead of the realities; her hearing was greatly impaired; her memory also; and her speech was unintelligible. When, at last, she came round so far as to be helped down stairs, it was still necessary to keep my slate always by her, that she might indicate in writing what she could not indicate in speech. As she was (very bad handwriting apart) a more than indifferent speller, and as Joe was a more than indifferent reader, extraordinary complications arose between them which I was always called

GREAT EXPECTATIONS
BY CHARLES DICKENS

# Create a poem about your Mother

For my own poor part, the fading summer left me out of health, out of spirits, and, if the truth must be told, out of money as well. During the past year I had not managed my professional resources as carefully as usual; and my extravagance now limited me to the prospect of spending the autumn economically between my mother's cottage at Hampstead and my own chambers in town. The evening, I remember, was still and cloudy; the London air was at its heaviest; the distant hum of the street-traffic was at its faintest; the small pulse of the life within me, and the great heart of the city around me, seemed to be sinking in unison, languidly and more languidly, with the sinking sun. I roused myself from the book which I was dreaming over rather than reading, and left my chambers to meet the cool night air in the suburbs. It was one of the two evenings in every week which I was accustomed to spend with my mother and my sister. So I turned my steps northward in the direction of Hampstead. Events which I have yet to relate make it necessary to mention in this place that my father had been dead some years at the period of which I am now writing; and that my sister Sarah and I were the sole survivors of a family of five children. My father was a drawing-master before me. His exertions had made him highly successful in his profession; and his affectionate anxiety to provide for the future of those who were dependent on his labours had impelled him, from the time of his marriage, to devote to the insuring of his life a much larger portion of his income than most men consider it necessary to set aside for that purpose. Thanks to his admirable prudence and self-denial my mother and sister were left, after his death, as independent of the world as they had been during his lifetime. I succeeded to his connection, and had every reason to feel grateful for the prospect that awaited me at my starting in life. The quiet twilight was still trembling on the topmost ridges of the heath; and the view of London below me had sunk into a black gulf in the shadow of the cloudy night, when I stood before the gate of my mother's cottage. I had hardly rung the bell before the house door was opened violently; my worthy Italian friend, Professor Pesca, appeared in the servant's place; and darted out joyously to receive me, with a shrill foreign parody on an English cheer. On his own account, and, I must be allowed to add, on mine also, the Professor merits the honour of a formal introduction. Accident has made him the starting-point of the strange family story

# THE WOMAN IN WHITE
## BY WILKIE COLLINS

# Create a poem about Birthdays

Three more birthdays of little Lucie had been woven by the golden thread into the peaceful tissue of the life of her home. Many a night and many a day had its inmates listened to the echoes in the corner, with hearts that failed them when they heard the thronging feet. For, the footsteps had become to their minds as the footsteps of a people, tumultuous under a red flag and with their country declared in danger, changed into wild beasts, by terrible enchantment long persisted in. Monseigneur, as a class, had dissociated himself from the phenomenon of his not being appreciated: of his being so little wanted in France, as to incur considerable danger of receiving his dismissal from it, and this life together. Like the fabled rustic who raised the Devil with infinite pains, and was so terrified at the sight of him that he could ask the Enemy no question, but immediately fled; so, Monseigneur, after boldly reading the Lord's Prayer backwards for a great number of years, and performing many other potent spells for compelling the Evil One, no sooner beheld him in his terrors than he took to his noble heels. The shining Bull's Eye of the Court was gone, or it would have been the mark for a hurricane of national bullets. It had never been a good eye to see with—had long had the mote in it of Lucifer's pride, Sardanapalus's luxury, and a mole's blindness—but it had dropped out and was gone. The Court, from that exclusive inner circle to its outermost rotten ring of intrigue, corruption, and dissimulation, was all gone together. Royalty was gone; had been besieged in its Palace and "suspended," when the last tidings came over. The August of the year one thousand seven hundred and ninety-two was come, and Monseigneur was by this time scattered far and wide. As was natural, the head-quarters and great gathering-place of Monseigneur, in London, was Tellson's Bank. Spirits are supposed to haunt the places where their bodies most resorted, and Monseigneur without a guinea haunted the spot where his guineas used to be. Moreover, it was the spot to which such French intelligence as was most to be relied upon, came quickest. Again: Tellson's was a munificent house, and extended great liberality to old customers who had fallen from their high estate. Again: those nobles who had seen the coming storm in time, and anticipating plunder or confiscation, had made provident remittances to Tellson's, were always to be heard of there by their needy brethren. To which it must be added that every new-comer from France reported himself and his tidings at

A TALE OF TWO CITIES
BY CHARLES DICKENS

# Create a poem about Friends

This table had a cover made out of beautiful oilcloth, with a red and blue spread-eagle painted on it, and a painted border all around. It come all the way from Philadelphia, they said. There was some books, too, piled up perfectly exact, on each corner of the table. One was a big family Bible full of pictures. One was Pilgrim's Progress, about a man that left his family, it didn't say why. I read considerable in it now and then. The statement was interesting, but tough. Another was Friendship's Offering, full of beautiful stuff and poetry; but I didn't read the poetry. Another was Henry Clay's Speeches, and another was Dr. Gunn's Family Medicine, which told you all about what to do if a body was sick or dead. There was a hymn book, and a lot of other books. And there was nice split-bottom chairs, and perfectly sound, too—not bagged down in the middle and busted, like an old basket. They had pictures hung on the walls—mainly Washington's and Lafayettes, and battles, and Highland Marys, and one called "Signing the Declaration." There was some that they called crayons, which one of the daughters which was dead made her own self when she was only fifteen years old. They was different from any pictures I ever see before—blacker, mostly, than is common. One was a woman in a slim black dress, belted small under the armpits, with bulges like a cabbage in the middle of the sleeves, and a large black scoop-shovel bonnet with a black veil, and white slim ankles crossed about with black tape, and very wee black slippers, like a chisel, and she was leaning pensive on a tombstone on her right elbow, under a weeping willow, and her other hand hanging down her side holding a white handkerchief and a reticule, and underneath the picture it said "Shall I Never See Thee More Alas." Another one was a young lady with her hair all combed up straight to the top of her head, and knotted there in front of a comb like a chair-back, and she was crying into a handkerchief and had a dead bird laying on its back in her other hand with its heels up, and underneath the picture it said "I Shall Never Hear Thy Sweet Chirrup More Alas." There was one where a young lady was at a window looking up at the moon, and tears running down her cheeks; and she had an open letter in one hand with black sealing wax showing on one edge of it, and she was mashing a locket with a chain to it against her mouth, and underneath the picture it said "And Art Thou Gone Yes Thou Art Gone Alas." These was all nice pictures, I reckon, but I didn't somehow seem to take to them, because

# ADVENTURES OF HUCKLEBERRY FINN
## BY MARK TWAIN

# Create a poem about Dawn

Becquer's prose is doubtless at its best in his letters entitled Desde mi Celda, written, as has been said, from the monastery of Veruela, in 1864. Read his description of his journey to the ancient Aragonese town of Tarazona, picturesquely situated on the River Queiles, of his mule trip over the glorious Moncayo, of the peacefulness and quiet of the old fortified monastery of Veruela, and you will surely feel inspired to follow him in his wanderings. Writing of his life in the seclusion of Veruela, Becquer says: "Every afternoon, as the sun is about to set, I sally forth upon the road that runs in front of the monastery doors to wait for the postman, who brings me the Madrid newspapers. In front of the archway that gives entrance to the first inclosure of the abbey stretches a long avenue of poplars so tall that when their branches are stirred by the evening breeze their summits touch and form an immense arch of verdure. On both sides of the road, leaping and tumbling with a pleasant murmur among the twisted roots of the trees, run two rivulets of crystalline transparent water, as cold as the blade of a sword and as gleaming as its edge. The ground, over which float the shadows of the poplars, mottled with restless spots of light, is covered at intervals with the thickest and finest of grass, in which grow so many white daisies that they look at first sight like that rain of petals with which the fruit-trees carpet the ground on warm April days. On the banks of the stream, amid the brambles and the reeds, grow wild violets, which, though well-nigh hidden amongst their creeping leaves, proclaim themselves afar by their penetrating perfume. And finally, also near the water and forming as it were a second boundary, can be seen between the poplar trunks a double row of stocky walnut-trees with dark, round, compact tops." About half way down the avenue stands a marble cross, which, from its color, is known in the vicinity as the Black Cross of Veruela. "Nothing is more somberly beautiful than this spot. At one end of the road the view is closed by the monastery, with its pointed arches, its peaked towers, and its imposing battlemented walls; on the other, the ruins of a little hermitage rise, at the foot of a hillock bestrewn with blooming thyme and rosemary. There, seated at the foot of the cross, and holding in my hands a book that I scarcely ever read and often leave forgotten on the steps of the cross, I linger for one, two, and sometimes even four hours waiting for the papers." At last the post arrives, and the Contemporáneo is in his hands. "As I was present at its birth,

LEGENDS, TALES AND POEMS
BY GUSTAVO ADOLFO BECQUER

# Create a poem about Sadness

"Since writing the above, dearest Lizzy, something has occurred of a most unexpected and serious nature; but I am afraid of alarming you—be assured that we are all well. What I have to say relates to poor Lydia. An express came at twelve last night, just as we were all gone to bed, from Colonel Forster, to inform us that she was gone off to Scotland with one of his officers; to own the truth, with Wickham! Imagine our surprise. To Kitty, however, it does not seem so wholly unexpected. I am very, very sorry. So imprudent a match on both sides! But I am willing to hope the best, and that his character has been misunderstood. Thoughtless and indiscreet I can easily believe him, but this step (and let us rejoice over it) marks nothing bad at heart. His choice is disinterested at least, for he must know my father can give her nothing. Our poor mother is sadly grieved. My father bears it better. How thankful am I that we never let them know what has been said against him; we must forget it ourselves. They were off Saturday night about twelve, as is conjectured, but were not missed till yesterday morning at eight. The express was sent off directly. My dear Lizzy, they must have passed within ten miles of us. Colonel Forster gives us reason to expect him here soon. Lydia left a few lines for his wife, informing her of their intention. I must conclude, for I cannot be long from my poor mother. I am afraid you will not be able to make it out, but I hardly know what I have written."Without allowing herself time for consideration, and scarcely knowing what she felt, Elizabeth on finishing this letter instantly seized the other, and opening it with the utmost impatience, read as follows: it had been written a day later than the conclusion of the first. "By this time, my dearest sister, you have received my hurried letter; I wish this may be more intelligible, but though not confined for time, my head is so bewildered that I cannot answer for being coherent. Dearest Lizzy, I hardly know what I would write, but I have bad news for you, and it cannot be delayed. Imprudent as the marriage between Mr. Wickham and our poor Lydia would be, we are now anxious to be assured it has taken place, for there is but too much reason to fear they are not gone to Scotland. Colonel Forster came yesterday, having left Brighton the day before, not many hours after the express. Though Lydia's short letter to Mrs. F. gave them to understand that they were going to Gretna Green, something was dropped by Denny expressing his belief that W. never intended to go there, or to marry Lydia at all,

**PRIDE AND PREJUDICE
BY JANE AUSTEN**

# Create a poem about Christmas

'Curiouser and curiouser!' cried Alice (she was so much surprised, that for the moment she quite forgot how to speak good English); 'now I'm opening out like the largest telescope that ever was! Good-bye, feet!' (for when she looked down at her feet, they seemed to be almost out of sight, they were getting so far off). 'Oh, my poor little feet, I wonder who will put on your shoes and stockings for you now, dears? I'm sure I shan't be able! I shall be a great deal too far off to trouble myself about you: you must manage the best way you can;—but I must be kind to them,' thought Alice, 'or perhaps they won't walk the way I want to go! Let me see: I'll give them a new pair of boots every Christmas.' And she went on planning to herself how she would manage it. 'They must go by the carrier,' she thought; 'and how funny it'll seem, sending presents to one's own feet! And how odd the directions will look! Oh dear, what nonsense I'm talking!' Just then her head struck against the roof of the hall: in fact she was now more than nine feet high, and she at once took up the little golden key and hurried off to the garden door. Poor Alice! It was as much as she could do, lying down on one side, to look through into the garden with one eye; but to get through was more hopeless than ever: she sat down and began to cry again. 'You ought to be ashamed of yourself,' said Alice, 'a great girl like you,' (she might well say this), 'to go on crying in this way! Stop this moment, I tell you!' But she went on all the same, shedding gallons of tears, until there was a large pool all round her, about four inches deep and reaching half down the hall. After a time she heard a little pattering of feet in the distance, and she hastily dried her eyes to see what was coming. It was the White Rabbit returning, splendidly dressed, with a pair of white kid gloves in one hand and a large fan in the other: he came trotting along in a great hurry, muttering to himself as he came, 'Oh! the Duchess, the Duchess! Oh! won't she be savage if I've kept her waiting!' Alice felt so desperate that she was ready to ask help of any one; so, when the Rabbit came near her, she began, in a low, timid voice, 'If you please, sir—' The Rabbit started violently, dropped the white kid gloves and the fan, and skurried away into the darkness as hard as he could go. Alice took up the fan and gloves, and, as the hall was very hot, she kept fanning herself all the time she went on talking: 'Dear, dear! How queer everything is to-day! And yesterday things went on just as usual. I wonder if I've been changed in the night? Let me think: was I the same when I got up this morning? I

# ALICE'S ADVENTURES IN WONDERLAND
# BY LEWIS CARROLL

# Create a poem about Dads

"Jack, I was so anxious. I read between the lines of your letter, and have been in an agony. The dad was better, so I ran down here to see for myself. Is not that gentleman Dr. Van Helsing? I am so thankful to you, sir, for coming." When first the Professor's eye had lit upon him he had been angry at his interruption at such a time; but now, as he took in his stalwart proportions and recognised the strong young manhood which seemed to emanate from him, his eyes gleamed. Without a pause he said to him gravely as he held out his hand:— "Sir, you have come in time. You are the lover of our dear miss. She is bad, very, very bad. Nay, my child, do not go like that." For he suddenly grew pale and sat down in a chair almost fainting. "You are to help her. You can do more than any that live, and your courage is your best help. "What can I do?" asked Arthur hoarsely. "Tell me, and I shall do it. My life is hers, and I would give the last drop of blood in my body for her." The Professor has a strongly humorous side, and I could from old knowledge detect a trace of its origin in his answer:— "My young sir, I do not ask so much as that—not the last!" "What shall I do?" There was fire in his eyes, and his open nostril quivered with intent. Van Helsing slapped him on the shoulder. "Come!" he said. "You are a man, and it is a man we want. You are better than me, better than my friend John." Arthur looked bewildered, and the Professor went on by explaining in a kindly way:— "Young miss is bad, very bad. She wants blood, and blood she must have or die. My friend John and I have consulted; and we are about to perform what we call transfusion of blood—to transfer from full veins of one to the empty veins which pine for him. John was to give his blood, as he is the more young and strong than me"—here Arthur took my hand and wrung it hard in silence—"but, now you are here, you are more good than us, old or young, who toil much in the world of thought. Our nerves are not so calm and our blood not so bright than yours!" Arthur turned to him and said:— "If you only knew how gladly I would die for her you would understand——" He stopped, with a sort of choke in his voice. "Good boy!" said Van Helsing. "In the not-so-far-off you will be happy that you have done all for her you love. Come now and be silent. You shall kiss her once before it is done, but then you must go; and you must leave at my sign. Say no word to Madame; you know how it is with her! There must be no shock; any knowledge of this would be one. Come!" We all went up to Lucy's room. Arthur by direction remained outside. Lucy turned her head and looked at us, but said nothing. She

DRACULA
BY BRAM STOKER

# Create a poem about Death

Stubb was the second mate. He was a native of Cape Cod; and hence, according to local usage, was called a Cape-Cod-man. A happy-go-lucky; neither craven nor valiant; taking perils as they came with an indifferent air; and while engaged in the most imminent crisis of the chase, toiling away, calm and collected as a journeyman joiner engaged for the year. Good-humored, easy, and careless, he presided over his whale-boat as if the most deadly encounter were but a dinner, and his crew all invited guests. He was as particular about the comfortable arrangement of his part of the boat, as an old stage-driver is about the snugness of his box. When close to the whale, in the very death-lock of the fight, he handled his unpitying lance coolly and off-handedly, as a whistling tinker his hammer. He would hum over his old rigadig tunes while flank and flank with the most exasperated monster. Long usage had, for this Stubb, converted the jaws of death into an easy chair. What he thought of death itself, there is no telling. Whether he ever thought of it at all, might be a question; but, if he ever did chance to cast his mind that way after a comfortable dinner, no doubt, like a good sailor, he took it to be a sort of call of the watch to tumble aloft, and bestir themselves there, about something which he would find out when he obeyed the order, and not sooner. What, perhaps, with other things, made Stubb such an easy-going, unfearing man, so cheerily trudging off with the burden of life in a world full of grave pedlars, all bowed to the ground with their packs; what helped to bring about that almost impious good-humor of his; that thing must have been his pipe. For, like his nose, his short, black little pipe was one of the regular features of his face. You would almost as soon have expected him to turn out of his bunk without his nose as without his pipe. He kept a whole row of pipes there ready loaded, stuck in a rack, within easy reach of his hand; and, whenever he turned in, he smoked them all out in succession, lighting one from the other to the end of the chapter; then loading them again to be in readiness anew. For, when Stubb dressed, instead of first putting his legs into his trowsers, he put his pipe into his mouth. I say this continual smoking must have been one cause, at least, of his peculiar disposition; for every one knows that this earthly air, whether ashore or afloat, is terribly infected with the nameless miseries of the numberless mortals who have died exhaling it; and as in time of the cholera, some people go about with a camphorated handkerchief to their mouths;

MOBY DICK; OR, THE WHALE
BY HERMAN MELVILLE

# Create a poem about Romance

The contents of these works are in themselves a literary curiosity. There are to be found both in Sanscrit poetry and in the Sanscrit drama a certain amount of poetical sentiment and romance, which have, in every country and in every language, thrown an immortal halo round the subject. But here it is treated in a plain, simple, matter of fact sort of way. Men and women are divided into classes and divisions in the same way that Buffon and other writers on natural history have classified and divided the animal world. As Venus was represented by the Greeks to stand forth as the type of the beauty of woman, so the Hindoos describe the Padmini or Lotus woman as the type of most perfect feminine excellence, as follows: She in whom the following signs and symptoms appear is called a Padmini. Her face is pleasing as the full moon; her body, well clothed with flesh, is soft as the Shiras or mustard[6] flower, her skin is fine, tender and fair as the yellow lotus, never dark coloured. Her eyes are bright and beautiful as the orbs of the fawn, well cut, and with reddish corners. Her bosom is hard, full and high; she has a good neck; her nose is straight and lovely, and three folds or wrinkles cross her middle—about the umbilical region. Her yoni resembles the opening lotus bud, and her love seed (Kama salila) is perfumed like the lily that has newly burst. She walks with swan-like gait, and her voice is low and musical as the note of the Kokila bird, she delights in white raiments, in fine jewels, and in rich dresses. She eats little, sleeps lightly, and being as respectful and religious as she is clever and courteous, she is ever anxious to worship the gods, and to enjoy the conversation of Brahmans. Such, then, is the Padmini or Lotus woman. Detailed descriptions then follow of the Chitrini or Art woman; the Shankhini or Conch woman, and the Hastini or Elephant woman, their days of enjoyment, their various seats of passion, the manner in which they should be manipulated and treated in sexual intercourse, along with the characteristics of the men and women of the various countries in Hindostan. The details are so numerous, and the subjects so seriously dealt with, and at such length, that neither time nor space will permit of their being given here. One work in the English language is somewhat similar to these works of the Hindoos. It is called 'Kalogynomia: or the Laws of Female Beauty,' being the elementary principles of that science, by T. Bell, M.D., with twenty-four plates, and printed in London in 1821. It treats of Beauty, of Love, of Sexual Intercourse, of the Laws

**THE KAMA SUTRA OF VATSYAYANA
BY VATSYAYANA**

# Create a poem about Nature

I have noted down what I have gained from their conversation, and have composed a small work on 'Principalities,' where I pour myself out as fully as I can in meditation on the subject, discussing what a principality is, what kinds there are, how they can be acquired, how they can be kept, why they are lost: and if any of my fancies ever pleased you, this ought not to displease you: and to a prince, especially to a new one, it should be welcome: therefore I dedicate it to his Magnificence Giuliano. Filippo Casavecchio has seen it; he will be able to tell you what is in it, and of the discourses I have had with him; nevertheless, I am still enriching and polishing it. "The "little book" suffered many vicissitudes before attaining the form in which it has reached us. Various mental influences were at work during its composition; its title and patron were changed; and for some unknown reason it was finally dedicated to Lorenzo de' Medici. Although Machiavelli discussed with Casavecchio whether it should be sent or presented in person to the patron, there is no evidence that Lorenzo ever received or even read it: he certainly never gave Machiavelli any employment. Although it was plagiarized during Machiavelli's lifetime, "The Prince" was never published by him, and its text is still disputable. Machiavelli concludes his letter to Vettori thus: "And as to this little thing [his book], when it has been read it will be seen that during the fifteen years I have given to the study of statecraft I have neither slept nor idled; and men ought ever to desire to be served by one who has reaped experience at the expense of others. And of my loyalty none could doubt, because having always kept faith I could not now learn how to break it; for he who has been faithful and honest, as I have, cannot change his nature; and my poverty is a witness to my honesty. "Before Machiavelli had got "The Prince" off his hands he commenced his "Discourse on the First Decade of Titus Livius," which should be read concurrently with "The Prince." These and several minor works occupied him until the year 1518, when he accepted a small commission to look after the affairs of some Florentine merchants at Genoa. In 1519 the Medicean rulers of Florence granted a few political concessions to her citizens, and Machiavelli with others was consulted upon a new constitution under which the Great Council was to be restored; but on one pretext or another it was not promulgated. In 1520 the Florentine merchants again had recourse to Machiavelli to settle their difficulties with

# THE PRINCE
## BY NICOLO MACHIAVELLI

# Create a poem about Dancing

As he jogged along over the fields, singing and dancing, a little dwarf met him, and asked him what made him so merry. 'Why, what should make me down-hearted?' said he; 'I am sound in health and rich in purse, what should I care for? I have saved up my three years' earnings and have it all safe in my pocket.' 'How much may it come to?' said the little man. 'Full threepence,' replied the countryman. 'I wish you would give them to me,' said the other; 'I am very poor.' Then the man pitied him, and gave him all he had; and the little dwarf said in return, 'As you have such a kind honest heart, I will grant you three wishes—one for every penny; so choose whatever you like.' Then the countryman rejoiced at his good luck, and said, 'I like many things better than money: first, I will have a bow that will bring down everything I shoot at; secondly, a fiddle that will set everyone dancing that hears me play upon it; and thirdly, I should like that everyone should grant what I ask.' The dwarf said he should have his three wishes; so he gave him the bow and fiddle, and went his way. Our honest friend journeyed on his way too; and if he was merry before, he was now ten times more so. He had not gone far before he met an old miser: close by them stood a tree, and on the topmost twig sat a thrush singing away most joyfully. 'Oh, what a pretty bird!' said the miser; 'I would give a great deal of money to have such a one.' 'If that's all,' said the countryman, 'I will soon bring it down.' Then he took up his bow, and down fell the thrush into the bushes at the foot of the tree. The miser crept into the bush to find it; but directly he had got into the middle, his companion took up his fiddle and played away, and the miser began to dance and spring about, capering higher and higher in the air. The thorns soon began to tear his clothes till they all hung in rags about him, and he himself was all scratched and wounded, so that the blood ran down. 'Oh, for heaven's sake!' cried the miser, 'Master! master! pray let the fiddle alone. What have I done to deserve this?' 'Thou hast shaved many a poor soul close enough,' said the other; 'thou art only meeting thy reward': so he played up another tune. Then the miser began to beg and promise, and offered money for his liberty; but he did not come up to the musician's price for some time, and he danced him along brisker and brisker, and the miser bid higher and higher, till at last he offered a round hundred of florins that he had in his purse, and had just gained by cheating some poor fellow. When the countryman saw so much money, he said, 'I will agree to your proposal.' So he took the purse, put up his

FAIRY TALES
BY THE BROTHERS GRIMM

# Create a poem about Laughter

The hybrid European—a tolerably ugly plebeian, taken all in all—absolutely requires a costume: he needs history as a storeroom of costumes. To be sure, he notices that none of the costumes fit him properly—he changes and changes. Let us look at the nineteenth century with respect to these hasty preferences and changes in its masquerades of style, and also with respect to its moments of desperation on account of "nothing suiting" us. It is in vain to get ourselves up as romantic, or classical, or Christian, or Florentine, or barocco, or "national," in moribus et artibus: it does not "clothe us"! But the "spirit," especially the "historical spirit," profits even by this desperation: once and again a new sample of the past or of the foreign is tested, put on, taken off, packed up, and above all studied—we are the first studious age in puncto of "costumes," I mean as concerns morals, articles of belief, artistic tastes, and religions; we are prepared as no other age has ever been for a carnival in the grand style, for the most spiritual festival—laughter and arrogance, for the transcendental height of supreme folly and Aristophanic ridicule of the world. Perhaps we are still discovering the domain of our invention just here, the domain where even we can still be original, probably as parodists of the world's history and as God's Merry-Andrews,—perhaps, though nothing else of the present have a future, our laughter itself may have a future! The historical sense (or the capacity for divining quickly the order of rank of the valuations according to which a people, a community, or an individual has lived, the "divining instinct" for the relationships of these valuations, for the relation of the authority of the valuations to the authority of the operating forces),—this historical sense, which we Europeans claim as our specialty, has come to us in the train of the enchanting and mad semi-barbarity into which Europe has been plunged by the democratic mingling of classes and races—it is only the nineteenth century that has recognized this faculty as its sixth sense. Owing to this mingling, the past of every form and mode of life, and of cultures which were formerly closely contiguous and superimposed on one another, flows forth into us "modern souls"; our instincts now run back in all directions, we ourselves are a kind of chaos: in the end, as we have said, the spirit perceives its advantage therein. By means of our semi-barbarity in body and in desire, we have secret access everywhere, such as a noble age never had; we have access

**BEYOND GOOD AND EVIL
BY FRIEDRICH NIETZSCHE**

# Create a poem about Words

"And yet," continued Lord Henry, in his low, musical voice, and with that graceful wave of the hand that was always so characteristic of him, and that he had even in his Eton days, "I believe that if one man were to live out his life fully and completely, were to give form to every feeling, expression to every thought, reality to every dream—I believe that the world would gain such a fresh impulse of joy that we would forget all the maladies of mediaevalism, and return to the Hellenic ideal—to something finer, richer than the Hellenic ideal, it may be. But the bravest man amongst us is afraid of himself. The mutilation of the savage has its tragic survival in the self-denial that mars our lives. We are punished for our refusals. Every impulse that we strive to strangle broods in the mind and poisons us. The body sins once, and has done with its sin, for action is a mode of purification. Nothing remains then but the recollection of a pleasure, or the luxury of a regret. The only way to get rid of a temptation is to yield to it. Resist it, and your soul grows sick with longing for the things it has forbidden to itself, with desire for what its monstrous laws have made monstrous and unlawful. It has been said that the great events of the world take place in the brain. It is in the brain, and the brain only, that the great sins of the world take place also. You, Mr. Gray, you yourself, with your rose-red youth and your rose-white boyhood, you have had passions that have made you afraid, thoughts that have filled you with terror, day-dreams and sleeping dreams whose mere memory might stain your cheek with shame—"Stop!" faltered Dorian Gray, "stop! you bewilder me. I don't know what to say. There is some answer to you, but I cannot find it. Don't speak. Let me think. Or, rather, let me try not to think. "For nearly ten minutes he stood there, motionless, with parted lips and eyes strangely bright. He was dimly conscious that entirely fresh influences were at work within him. Yet they seemed to him to have come really from himself. The few words that Basil's friend had said to him—words spoken by chance, no doubt, and with wilful paradox in them—had touched some secret chord that had never been touched before, but that he felt was now vibrating and throbbing to curious pulses.  Music had stirred him like that. Music had troubled him many times. But music was not articulate. It was not a new world, but rather another chaos, that it created in us. Words! Mere words! How terrible they were! How clear, and vivid, and cruel! One could not escape from them. And yet what a subtle

THE PICTURE OF DORIAN GRAY
BY OSCAR WILDE

# Create a poem about Beauty

The queen mother appealed to Paris to obtain 200,000 crowns, and a royal edict commanded the clergy to contribute 100,000 écus de rentes annual revenue.[713] At the same time a government octroi upon wines was laid for six years, to the dismay of many towns, which opposed the execution of the edict, claiming that the vine and wine were their sole means of livelihood.[714] The King also went to Parlement to obtain pecuniary supplies there against England, saying that the 200,000 crowns from the city was to be used to pay the reiters of the Rhinegrave, who had mutinied for their pay in Champagne, to quit the kingdom.[715] Paris readily responded, "the Parisians caring not what they gave to recover Newhaven;" it had been "a scourge and loss to them of many millions of francs" during that year. Meanwhile the position of Warwick in Havre had grown so[201] bad that he had expelled all strangers from the town.[717] Anticipating a siege, a new fosse 30 feet wide, 10 feet broad, and 8 feet deep had been constructed outside of the old ditch around the town. The delay of the English government, however, was fatal to the success of Warwick. All his labors went for naught.[718] On May 22 the French assault upon Havre began in earnest.[719] In the midst of the tedium and the anxiety Catherine de Medici dominated all, having no regard for her own convenience, but being in vigorous action at all hours, and under great mental strain most of the time. Yet her patience, her address, and her assiduous attention during the time of the siege to the councils of the government, and to her continual audiences, were remarkable. "Her Majesty," wrote the Venetian ambassador, "exceeds all that could be expected from her sex, and even from an experienced man of valor, or from a powerful king and military captain." She insisted on being present at all the assaults, and even in the trenches, where cannon-balls and arquebus-bullets were flying.[720] The character of Catherine de Medici from this time forth, throughout her long and varied career, continued to fill her subjects with astonishment. Not even the most consummate courtier[202] could have praised her beauty. She had big eyes and thick lips, like Leo X, her great-uncle.[721] She possessed, too, the characteristics of her family. She loved to erect public edifices; to collect books. She made a profession of satisfying everybody, at least in words, of which she was not saving. Her industry in public business was the subject of astonishment. Nothing was too small for her notice. She could neither eat nor drink without talking politics. She

# THE WARS OF RELIGION IN FRANCE
## BY JAMES WESTFALL THOMPSON, PH.D.

# Create a poem about Solitude

Holmes grinned at the last item. "Well," he said, "I say now, as I said then, that a man should keep his little brain-attic stocked with all the furniture that he is likely to use, and the rest he can put away in the lumber-room of his library, where he can get it if he wants it. Now, for such a case as the one which has been submitted to us to-night, we need certainly to muster all our resources. Kindly hand me down the letter K of the American Encyclopaedia which stands upon the shelf beside you. Thank you. Now let us consider the situation and see what may be deduced from it. In the first place, we may start with a strong presumption that Colonel Openshaw had some very strong reason for leaving America. Men at his time of life do not change all their habits and exchange willingly the charming climate of Florida for the lonely life of an English provincial town. His extreme love of solitude in England suggests the idea that he was in fear of someone or something, so we may assume as a working hypothesis that it was fear of someone or something which drove him from America. As to what it was he feared, we can only deduce that by considering the formidable letters which were received by himself and his successors. Did you remark the postmarks of those letters? "The first was from Pondicherry, the second from Dundee, and the third from London. "From East London. What do you deduce from that?" "They are all seaports. That the writer was on board of a ship. "Excellent. We have already a clue. There can be no doubt that the probability—the strong probability—is that the writer was on board of a ship. And now let us consider another point. In the case of Pondicherry, seven weeks elapsed between the threat and its fulfilment, in Dundee it was only some three or four days. Does that suggest anything?" "A greater distance to travel. "But the letter had also a greater distance to come." "Then I do not see the point." "There is at least a presumption that the vessel in which the man or men are is a sailing-ship. It looks as if they always send their singular warning or token before them when starting upon their mission. You see how quickly the deed followed the sign when it came from Dundee. If they had come from Pondicherry in a steamer they would have arrived almost as soon as their letter. But, as a matter of fact, seven weeks elapsed. I think that those seven weeks represented the difference between the mail-boat which brought the letter and the sailing vessel which brought the writer." "It is possible." "More than that. It is probable. And now you see

# THE ADVENTURES OF SHERLOCK HOLMES
## BY SIR ARTHUR CONAN DOYLE

# Create a poem about Tenderness

Tenors get women by the score. Increase their flow. Throw flower at his feet. When will we meet? My head it simply. Jingle all delighted. He can't sing for tall hats. Your head it simply swurls. Perfumed for him. What perfume does your wife? I want to know. Jing. Stop. Knock. Last look at mirror always before she answers the door. The hall. There? How do you? I do well. There? What? Or? Phial of cachous, kissing comfits, in her satchel. Yes? Hands felt for the opulent. Alas the voice rose, sighing, changed: loud, full, shining, proud. —But alas, 'twas idle dreaming... Glorious tone he has still. Cork air softer also their brogue. Silly man! Could have made oceans of money. Singing wrong words. Wore out his wife: now sings. But hard to tell. Only the two themselves. If he doesn't break down. Keep a trot for the avenue. His hands and feet sing too. Drink. Nerves overstrung. Must be abstemious to sing. Jenny Lind soup: stock, sage, raw eggs, half pint of cream. For creamy dreamy. Tenderness it welled: slow, swelling, full it throbbed. That's the chat. Ha, give! Take! Throb, a throb, a pulsing proud erect. Words? Music? No: it's what's behind. Bloom looped, unlooped, noded, disnoded. Bloom. Flood of warm jamjam lickitup secretness flowed to flow in music out, in desire, dark to lick flow invading. Tipping her tepping her tapping her topping her. Tup. Pores to dilate dilating. Tup. The joy the feel the warm the. Tup. To pour o'er sluices pouring gushes. Flood, gush, flow, joygush, tupthrob. Now! Language of love. —... ray of hope is... Beaming. Lydia for Lidwell squeak scarcely hear so ladylike the muse unsqueaked a ray of hopk. Martha it is. Coincidence. Just going to write. Lionel's song. Lovely name you have. Can't write. Accept my little pres. Play on her heartstrings pursestrings too. She's a. I called you naughty boy. Still the name: Martha. How strange! Today. The voice of Lionel returned, weaker but unwearied. It sang again to Richie Poldy Lydia Lidwell also sang to Pat open mouth ear waiting to wait. How first he saw that form endearing, how sorrow seemed to part, how look, form, word charmed him Gould Lidwell, won Pat Bloom's heart. Wish I could see his face, though. Explain better. Why the barber in Drago's always looked my face when I spoke his face in the glass. Still hear it better here than in the bar though farther. —Each graceful look... First night when first I saw her at Mat Dillon's in Terenure. Yellow, black lace she wore. Musical chairs. We two the last. Fate. After her. Fate. Round and round slow. Quick round. We two. All looked. Halt. Down she

# Create a poem about Creativity

Salnis became more and more animated. "Do you know how I picture God myself?" he said. "As an enormous, creative organ beyond our ken, who scatters millions of worlds into space, just as one single fish would deposit its spawn in the sea. He creates because it is His function as God to do so, but He does not know what He is doing and is stupidly prolific in His work and is ignorant of the combinations of all kinds which are produced by His scattered germs. The human mind is a lucky little local, passing accident which was totally unforeseen, and condemned to disappear with this earth and to recommence perhaps here or elsewhere the same or different with fresh combinations of eternally new beginnings. We owe it to this little lapse of intelligence on His part that we are very uncomfortable in this world which was not made for us, which had not been prepared to receive us, to lodge and feed us or to satisfy reflecting beings, and we owe it to Him also that we have to struggle without ceasing against what are still called the designs of Providence, when we are really refined and civilized beings. "Grandin, who was listening to him attentively as he had long known the surprising outbursts of his imagination, asked him: "Then you believe that human thought is the spontaneous product of blind divine generation? "Naturally! A fortuitous function of the nerve centres of our brain, like the unforeseen chemical action due to new mixtures and similar also to a charge of electricity, caused by friction or the unexpected proximity of some substance, similar to all phenomena caused by the infinite and fruitful fermentation of living matter. "But, my dear fellow, the truth of this must be evident to any one who looks about him. If the human mind, ordained by an omniscient Creator, had been intended to be what it has become, exacting, inquiring, agitated, tormented—so different from mere animal thought and resignation—would the world which was created to receive the beings which we now are have been this unpleasant little park for small game, this salad patch, this wooded, rocky and spherical kitchen garden where your improvident Providence had destined us to live naked, in caves or under trees, nourished on the flesh of slaughtered animals, our brethren, or on raw vegetables nourished by the sun and the rain? "But it is sufficient to reflect for a moment, in order to understand that this world was not made for such creatures as we are. Thought, which is developed by a miracle in the nerves of the cells in our brain, powerless,

MAUPASSANT ORIGINAL SHORT STORIES
BY GUY DE MAUPASSANT

# Create a poem about Darkness

All these, however, were mere terrors of the night, phantoms of the mind that walk in darkness; and though he had seen many spectres in his time, and been more than once beset by Satan in divers shapes, in his lonely perambulations, yet daylight put an end to all these evils; and he would have passed a pleasant life of it, in despite of the Devil and all his works, if his path had not been crossed by a being that causes more perplexity to mortal man than ghosts, goblins, and the whole race of witches put together, and that was—a woman. Among the musical disciples who assembled, one evening in each week, to receive his instructions in psalmody, was Katrina Van Tassel, the daughter and only child of a substantial Dutch farmer. She was a blooming lass of fresh eighteen; plump as a partridge; ripe and melting and rosy-cheeked as one of her father's peaches, and universally famed, not merely for her beauty, but her vast expectations. She was withal a little of a coquette, as might be perceived even in her dress, which was a mixture of ancient and modern fashions, as most suited to set off her charms. She wore the ornaments of pure yellow gold, which her great-great-grandmother had brought over from Saardam; the tempting stomacher of the olden time, and withal a provokingly short petticoat, to display the prettiest foot and ankle in the country round. Ichabod Crane had a soft and foolish heart towards the sex; and it is not to be wondered at that so tempting a morsel soon found favor in his eyes, more especially after he had visited her in her paternal mansion. Old Baltus Van Tassel was a perfect picture of a thriving, contented, liberal-hearted farmer. He seldom, it is true, sent either his eyes or his thoughts beyond the boundaries of his own farm; but within those everything was snug, happy and well-conditioned. He was satisfied with his wealth, but not proud of it; and piqued himself upon the hearty abundance, rather than the style in which he lived. His stronghold was situated on the banks of the Hudson, in one of those green, sheltered, fertile nooks in which the Dutch farmers are so fond of nestling. A great elm tree spread its broad branches over it, at the foot of which bubbled up spring of the softest and sweetest water, in a little well formed of a barrel; and then stole sparkling away through the grass, to a neighboring brook, that babbled along among alders and dwarf willows. Hard by the farmhouse was a vast barn, that might have served for a church; every window and crevice of which seemed bursting forth with the treasures of the

# THE LEGEND OF SLEEPY HOLLOW
## BY WASHINGTON IRVING

# Create a poem about Joy

I was astounded. The Prefect appeared absolutely thunder-stricken. For some minutes he remained speechless and motionless, looking incredulously at my friend with open mouth, and eyes that seemed starting from their sockets; then, apparently recovering himself in some measure, he seized a pen, and after several pauses and vacant stares, finally filled up and signed a check for fifty thousand francs, and handed it across the table to Dupin. The latter examined it carefully and deposited it in his pocket-book; then, unlocking an escritoire, took thence a letter and gave it to the Prefect. This functionary grasped it in a perfect agony of joy, opened it with a trembling hand, cast a rapid glance at its contents, and then, scrambling and struggling to the door, rushed at length unceremoniously from the room and from the house, without having uttered a syllable since Dupin had requested him to fill up the check. When he had gone, my friend entered into some explanations. "The Parisian police," he said, "are exceedingly able in their way. They are persevering, ingenious, cunning, and thoroughly versed in the knowledge which their duties seem chiefly to demand. Thus, when G— detailed to us his mode of searching the premises at the Hotel D—, I felt entire confidence in his having made a satisfactory investigation—so far as his labors extended. "So far as his labors extended?" said I. "Yes," said Dupin. "The measures adopted were not only the best of their kind, but carried out to absolute perfection. Had the letter been deposited within the range of their search, these fellows would, beyond a question, have found it. "I merely laughed—but he seemed quite serious in all that he said. "The measures, then," he continued, "were good in their kind, and well executed; their defect lay in their being inapplicable to the case, and to the man. A certain set of highly ingenious resources are, with the Prefect, a sort of Procrustean bed, to which he forcibly adapts his designs. But he perpetually errs by being too deep or too shallow, for the matter in hand; and many a schoolboy is a better reasoner than he. I knew one about eight years of age, whose success at guessing in the game of 'even and odd' attracted universal admiration. This game is simple, and is played with marbles. One player holds in his hand a number of these toys, and demands of another whether that number is even or odd. If the guess is right, the guesser wins one; if wrong, he loses one. The boy to whom I allude won all the marbles of the school. Of course he had some principle of

**THE WORKS OF EDGAR ALLEN POE**
**BY EDGAR ALLEN POE**

# Create a poem about Desire

Yes, let me acknowledge that on this first day I let the charm of her presence lure me from the recollection of myself and my position. The most trifling of the questions that she put to me, on the subject of using her pencil and mixing her colours; the slightest alterations of expression in the lovely eyes that looked into mine with such an earnest desire to learn all that I could teach, and to discover all that I could show, attracted more of my attention than the finest view we passed through, or the grandest changes of light and shade, as they flowed into each other over the waving moorland and the level beach. At any time, and under any circumstances of human interest, is it not strange to see how little real hold the objects of the natural world amid which we live can gain on our hearts and minds? We go to Nature for comfort in trouble, and sympathy in joy, only in books. Admiration of those beauties of the inanimate world, which modern poetry so largely and so eloquently describes, is not, even in the best of us, one of the original instincts of our nature. As children, we none of us possess it. No uninstructed man or woman possesses it. Those whose lives are most exclusively passed amid the ever-changing wonders of sea and land are also those who are most universally insensible to every aspect of Nature not directly associated with the human interest of their calling. Our capacity of appreciating the beauties of the earth we live on is, in truth, one of the civilised accomplishments which we all learn as an Art; and, more, that very capacity is rarely practised by any of us except when our minds are most indolent and most unoccupied. How much share have the attractions of Nature ever had in the pleasurable or painful interests and emotions of ourselves or our friends? What space do they ever occupy in the thousand little narratives of personal experience which pass every day by word of mouth from one of us to the other? All that our minds can compass, all that our hearts can learn, can be accomplished with equal certainty, equal profit, and equal satisfaction to ourselves, in the poorest as in the richest prospect that the face of the earth can show. There is surely a reason for this want of inborn sympathy between the creature and the creation around it, a reason which may perhaps be found in the widely-differing destinies of man and his earthly sphere. The grandest mountain prospect that the eye can range over is appointed to annihilation. The smallest human interest that the pure heart can feel is appointed to

# THE WOMAN IN WHITE
## BY WILKIE COLLINS

# Create a poem about Hands

Perhaps it had originally been their design to make use of the rope in order to stop the pay car. The discovery of an overturned sapling however had suggested an easier method of proceeding. Bill hastened to arrange a loop at one end of the rope. This he passed over the head of the boy, and the touch of the noose on his face sent a cold chill all through the body of the helpless prisoner. "Fix it just under his arms, Bill," commanded the tall man. "I warn you to keep still, younker, if you know what's best for you. No matter what you say, or try to do, you can't change our plans. We mean to keep you here, so as to hold back the alarm as long as we can, which'll give us a chance to cover many miles, if your dinky old car holds out. Now, walk over here with us, and you'll grip on what the scheme is." With one on either side Gusty was compelled to advance, and he noted with considerable trepidation that it was directly toward the precipice that they led him. "You wouldn't hang me over there like this, would you?" he ejaculated, as a terrible thought flashed into his mind. "Why, before long this rope would cut into me so I'd be crazy with pain. Tie me to a tree if you want, so I can't get away, but don't put me over there, please!" It would have to be something beyond the common that could make a proud boy like Gusty Merrivale plead with anyone; but for the time being he forgot his haughty spirit, nor was it to be wondered at, considering the peril he faced. "No use wastin' yer breath, kid," snarled the shorter hobo. "We laid out our plans an' we means tuh kerry the same through, don't we, Pete?" "It ain't quite as bad as you thinks, younker," added the other man, who seemed to have just a grain of pity in his nature. "'Bout twelve or fifteen feet down the face of the precipice there's a ledge that runs along a little ways. No goat could ever get up or down from that same place. We're meaning to land you there, drop the short rope, and leave you till somebody happens to come along, which might be in one hour, and mebbe not till night sets in. The rope is ten times too short for you to use it in lowering yourself down, so you've just got to hold the fort. Now, lay back, and no kicking remember, because you might make us let go, and that'd mean a tumble on the rocks two hundred feet below here. Steady now, Bill, wait till I give the word, and lower away slow like. Make the best of a bad bargain, younker. Remember, we might a done worse by you." Afraid to struggle, and holding his very breath with dreadful suspense, the boy felt himself being lowered through empty space. He could look far down toward the

THE BOY SCOUTS IN THE SADDLE
BY ROBERT SHALER

# Create a poem about Eyes

Mrs. Pontellier's eyes were quick and bright; they were a yellowish brown, about the color of her hair. She had a way of turning them swiftly upon an object and holding them there as if lost in some inward maze of contemplation or thought. Her eyebrows were a shade darker than her hair. They were thick and almost horizontal, emphasizing the depth of her eyes. She was rather handsome than beautiful. Her face was captivating by reason of a certain frankness of expression and a contradictory subtle play of features. Her manner was engaging. Robert rolled a cigarette. He smoked cigarettes because he could not afford cigars, he said. He had a cigar in his pocket which Mr. Pontellier had presented him with, and he was saving it for his after-dinner smoke. This seemed quite proper and natural on his part. In coloring he was not unlike his companion. A clean-shaved face made the resemblance more pronounced than it would otherwise have been. There rested no shadow of care upon his open countenance. His eyes gathered in and reflected the light and languor of the summer day. Mrs. Pontellier reached over for a palm-leaf fan that lay on the porch and began to fan herself, while Robert sent between his lips light puffs from his cigarette. They chatted incessantly: about the things around them; their amusing adventure out in the water—it had again assumed its entertaining aspect; about the wind, the trees, the people who had gone to the Cheniere; about the children playing croquet under the oaks, and the Farival twins, who were now performing the overture to "The Poet and the Peasant." Robert talked a good deal about himself. He was very young, and did not know any better. Mrs. Pontellier talked a little about herself for the same reason. Each was interested in what the other said. Robert spoke of his intention to go to Mexico in the autumn, where fortune awaited him. He was always intending to go to Mexico, but some way never got there. Meanwhile he held on to his modest position in a mercantile house in New Orleans, where an equal familiarity with English, French and Spanish gave him no small value as a clerk and correspondent. He was spending his summer vacation, as he always did, with his mother at Grand Isle. In former times, before Robert could remember, "the house" had been a summer luxury of the Lebruns. Now, flanked by its dozen or more cottages, which were always filled with exclusive visitors from the "Quartier Francais," it enabled Madame Lebrun to maintain the easy and comfortable existence which appeared to be her

# THE AWAKENING AND SELECTED SHORT STORIES
## BY KATE CHOPIN

# Create a poem about Loss

The fear that the education of woman, in connection with her growing economic independence, will prove harmful to society through her refusal of matrimony or maternity appears equally groundless. According to Dike, "the demand for her enfranchisement, either as a right or on the ground of expediency, grows out of this way of treating her as an individual whose relations to society are less a matter of condition and more of personal choice. And this principle is carried into a sphere entirely her own. A partial loss of capacity for maternity has, it is said, already befallen American women; and the voluntary refusal of its responsibilities is the lament of the physician and the moralist."[815] It is true that the birth-rate is falling.[816] So far as this depends upon male sensuality, a prevalent cause of sterility; upon selfish love of ease and luxury—of which men even more than women are guilty; or upon the disastrous influence of the[243] present extremes of wealth and poverty—of which women as well as men are the victims—it is a serious evil which may well cause us anxiety; but so far as it is the result of the desire for fewer but better-born children—for which, let us hope, the advancing culture of woman may in part be responsible—it is in fact a positive social good.[817] It is true also that, while fewer and fewer marriages in proportion to the population are taking place, men as well as women are marrying later and later in life.[818] Here again, for the reasons just mentioned, the results are both good and bad. Certain it is that early marriages and excessive child-bearing have been the twin causes of much injury to the human race. "To the superficial observer," declares a writer very conservative as to the effects of woman's emancipation, "it may appear that every marriage must enrich the state, and that early marriages must lessen the amount of sexual immorality, but inquiry will prove conclusively how fallacious are those views. Early marriages certainly tend to the production of large families, but then a family, to be a source of wealth to the state, must at least be self-supporting, which is exactly what the feeble, degenerate children of the great mass of our early marriages are not. They are brought forth ill-developed and unhealthy; their immature, improvident parents are unable to either feed or educate them as they ought to be fed and educated; hence, instead of being a source of wealth to the state, they prove a serious drain upon her resources. A large percentage of these miserable

# A HISTORY OF MATRIMONIAL INSTITUTIONS
## BY GEORGE ELLIOTT HOWARD PH.D.

# Create a poem about Taste

"Well, did you find Diana a kindred spirit?" asked Marilla as they went up through the garden of Green Gables. "Oh yes," sighed Anne, blissfully unconscious of any sarcasm on Marilla's part. "Oh Marilla, I'm the happiest girl on Prince Edward Island this very moment. I assure you I'll say my prayers with a right good-will tonight. Diana and I are going to build a playhouse in Mr. William Bell's birch grove tomorrow. Can I have those broken pieces of china that are out in the woodshed? Diana's birthday is in February and mine is in March. Don't you think that is a very strange coincidence? Diana is going to lend me a book to read. She says it's perfectly splendid and tremendously exciting. She's going to show me a place back in the woods where rice lilies grow. Don't you think Diana has got very soulful eyes? I wish I had soulful eyes. Diana is going to teach me to sing a song called 'Nelly in the Hazel Dell.' She's going to give me a picture to put up in my room; it's a perfectly beautiful picture, she says—a lovely lady in a pale blue silk dress. A sewing-machine agent gave it to her. I wish I had something to give Diana. I'm an inch taller than Diana, but she is ever so much fatter; she says she'd like to be thin because it's so much more graceful, but I'm afraid she only said it to soothe my feelings. We're going to the shore some day to gather shells. We have agreed to call the spring down by the log bridge the Dryad's Bubble. Isn't that a perfectly elegant name? I read a story once about a spring called that. A dryad is sort of a grown-up fairy, I think."Well, all I hope is you won't talk Diana to death," said Marilla. "But remember this in all your planning, Anne. You're not going to play all the time nor most of it. You'll have your work to do and it'll have to be done first. "Anne's cup of happiness was full, and Matthew caused it to overflow. He had just got home from a trip to the store at Carmody, and he sheepishly produced a small parcel from his pocket and handed it to Anne, with a deprecatory look at Marilla. "I heard you say you liked chocolate sweeties, so I got you some," he said. "Humph," sniffed Marilla. "It'll ruin her teeth and stomach. There, there, child, don't look so dismal. You can eat those, since Matthew has gone and got them. He'd better have brought you peppermints. They're wholesomer. Don't sicken yourself eating all them at once now. "Oh, no, indeed, I won't," said Anne eagerly. "I'll just eat one tonight, Marilla. And I can give Diana half of them, can't I? The other half will taste twice as sweet to me if I give some to her. It's delightful to think I have something to give her. "I will

ANNE OF GREEN GABLES
BY LUCY MAUD MONTGOMERY

# Create a poem about Madness

Rhea, the wife of Cronus, and mother of Zeus and the other great gods of Olympus, personified the earth, and was regarded as the Great Mother and unceasing producer of all plant-life. She was also believed to exercise unbounded sway over the animal creation, more especially over the lion, the noble king of beasts. Rhea is generally represented wearing a crown of turrets or towers and seated on a throne, with lions crouching at her feet. She is sometimes depicted sitting in a chariot, drawn by lions.The principal seat of her worship, which was always of a very riotous character, was at Crete. At her festivals, which took place at night, the wildest music of flutes, cymbals, and drums resounded, whilst joyful shouts and cries, accompanied by dancing and loud stamping of feet, filled the air. This divinity was introduced into Crete by its first colonists from Phrygia, in Asia Minor, in which country she was worshipped under the name of Cybele. The people of Crete adored her as the Great Mother, more especially in her signification as the sustainer of the vegetable world. Seeing, however, that year by year, as winter appears, all her glory vanishes, her flowers fade, and her trees become leafless, they poetically expressed this process of nature under the figure of a lost love. She [19]was said to have been tenderly attached to a youth of remarkable beauty, named Atys, who, to her grief and indignation, proved faithless to her. He was about to unite himself to a nymph called Sagaris, when, in the midst of the wedding feast, the rage of the incensed goddess suddenly burst forth upon all present. A panic seized the assembled guests, and Atys, becoming afflicted with temporary madness, fled to the mountains and destroyed himself. Cybele, moved with sorrow and regret, instituted a yearly mourning for his loss, when her priests, the Corybantes, with their usual noisy accompaniments, marched into the mountains to seek the lost youth. Having discovered him[6] they gave full vent to their ecstatic delight by indulging in the most violent gesticulations, dancing, shouting, and, at the same time, wounding and gashing themselves in a frightful manner. In Rome the Greek Rhea was identified with Ops, the goddess of plenty, the wife of Saturn, who had a variety of appellations. She was called Magna-Mater, Mater-Deorum, Berecynthia-Idea, and also Dindymene. This latter title she acquired from three high mountains in Phrygia, whence she was brought to Rome as Cybele during the second Punic war, B.C. 205, in obedience to an injunction contained in the Sybilline books.

MYTHS AND LEGENDS OF ANCIENT
GREECE AND ROME.
BY E. M. BERENS.

# Create a poem about Age

Alice was just beginning to say 'There's a mistake somewhere—,' when the Queen began screaming so loud that she had to leave the sentence unfinished. 'Oh, oh, oh!' shouted the Queen, shaking her hand about as if she wanted to shake it off. 'My finger's bleeding! Oh, oh, oh, oh!' Her screams were so exactly like the whistle of a steam-engine, that Alice had to hold both her hands over her ears. 'What IS the matter?' she said, as soon as there was a chance of making herself heard. 'Have you pricked your finger?' 'I haven't pricked it YET,' the Queen said, 'but I soon shall—oh, oh, oh!' 'When do you expect to do it?' Alice asked, feeling very much inclined to laugh. 'When I fasten my shawl again,' the poor Queen groaned out: 'the brooch will come undone directly. Oh, oh!' As she said the words the brooch flew open, and the Queen clutched wildly at it, and tried to clasp it again. 'Take care!' cried Alice. 'You're holding it all crooked!' And she caught at the brooch; but it was too late: the pin had slipped, and the Queen had pricked her finger. 'That accounts for the bleeding, you see,' she said to Alice with a smile. 'Now you understand the way things happen here.' 'But why don't you scream now?' Alice asked, holding her hands ready to put over her ears again. 'Why, I've done all the screaming already,' said the Queen. 'What would be the good of having it all over again?' By this time it was getting light. 'The crow must have flown away, I think,' said Alice: 'I'm so glad it's gone. I thought it was the night coming on.' 'I wish I could manage to be glad!' the Queen said. 'Only I never can remember the rule. You must be very happy, living in this wood, and being glad whenever you like!' 'Only it is so VERY lonely here!' Alice said in a melancholy voice; and at the thought of her loneliness two large tears came rolling down her cheeks. 'Oh, don't go on like that!' cried the poor Queen, wringing her hands in despair. 'Consider what a great girl you are. Consider what a long way you've come to-day. Consider what o'clock it is. Consider anything, only don't cry!' Alice could not help laughing at this, even in the midst of her tears. 'Can YOU keep from crying by considering things?' she asked. 'That's the way it's done,' the Queen said with great decision: 'nobody can do two things at once, you know. Let's consider your age to begin with—how old are you?' 'I'm seven and a half exactly.' 'You needn't say "exactually,"' the Queen remarked: 'I can believe it without that. Now I'll give YOU something to believe. I'm just one hundred and one, five months and a day.' 'I can't believe THAT!' said Alice. 'Can't you?' the Queen said in a pitying

# Create a poem the Future

"No; not over exactly, but the future is yours, and the present is mine, and the present—well, it's not all that it might be. "How so?" "Oh, things go wrong. But I don't want to talk of myself, and besides I can't explain it all," said Stepan Arkadyevitch. "Well, why have you come to Moscow, then?.... Hi! take away!" he called to the Tatar. "You guess?" responded Levin, his eyes like deep wells of light fixed on Stepan Arkadyevitch. "I guess, but I can't be the first to talk about it. You can see by that whether I guess right or wrong," said Stepan Arkadyevitch, gazing at Levin with a subtle smile. "Well, and what have you to say to me?" said Levin in a quivering voice, feeling that all the muscles of his face were quivering too. "How do you look at the question?" Stepan Arkadyevitch slowly emptied his glass of Chablis, never taking his eyes off Levin. "I?" said Stepan Arkadyevitch, "there's nothing I desire so much as that—nothing! It would be the best thing that could be." "But you're not making a mistake? You know what we're speaking of?" said Levin, piercing him with his eyes. "You think it's possible?" "I think it's possible. Why not possible?" "No! do you really think it's possible? No, tell me all you think! Oh, but if ... if refusal's in store for me!... Indeed I feel sure..." "Why should you think that?" said Stepan Arkadyevitch, smiling at his excitement. "It seems so to me sometimes. That will be awful for me, and for her too." "Oh, well, anyway there's nothing awful in it for a girl. Every girl's proud of an offer." "Yes, every girl, but not she." Stepan Arkadyevitch smiled. He so well knew that feeling of Levin's, that for him all the girls in the world were divided into two classes: one class—all the girls in the world except her, and those girls with all sorts of human weaknesses, and very ordinary girls: the other class—she alone, having no weaknesses of any sort and higher than all humanity. "Stay, take some sauce," he said, holding back Levin's hand as it pushed away the sauce. Levin obediently helped himself to sauce, but would not let Stepan Arkadyevitch go on with his dinner. "No, stop a minute, stop a minute," he said. "You must understand that it's a question of life and death for me. I have never spoken to any one of this. And there's no one I could speak of it to, except you. You know we're utterly unlike each other, different tastes and views and everything; but I know you're fond of me and understand me, and that's why I like you awfully. But for God's sake, be quite straightforward with me." "I tell you what I think," said Stepan Arkadyevitch,

ANNA KARENINA
BY LEO TOLSTOY

# Create a poem about Forgiveness

"AH, Miss Everdene!" said the sergeant, touching his diminutive cap. "Little did I think it was you I was speaking to the other night. And yet, if I had reflected, the "Queen of the Corn-market" (truth is truth at any hour of the day or night, and I heard you so named in Casterbridge yesterday), the "Queen of the Corn-market." I say, could be no other woman. I step across now to beg your forgiveness a thousand times for having been led by my feelings to express myself too strongly for a stranger. To be sure I am no stranger to the place — I am Sergeant Troy, as I told you, and I have assisted your uncle in these fields no end of times when I was a lad. I have been doing the same for you today." "I suppose I must thank you for that, Sergeant Troy." said the Queen of the Corn-market, in an in- differently grateful tone. The sergeant looked hurt and sad. "Indeed you must not, Miss Everdene." he said. "Why could you think such a thing necessary?" "I am glad it is not." "Why? if I may ask without offence." "Because I don't much want to thank you for any" thing." "I am afraid I have made a hole with my tongue that my heart will never mend. O these intolerable times: that ill-luck should follow a man for honestly telling a woman she is beautiful! 'Twas the most I said — you must own that; and the least I could say — that I own myself." "There is some talk I could do without more easily than money." "Indeed. That remark is a sort of digression." "No. It means that I would rather have your room than your company." "And I would rather have curses from you than kisses from any other woman; so I'll stay here." Bathsheba was absolutely speechless. And yet she could not help feeling that the assistance he was render- ing forbade a harsh repulse. "Well." continued Troy, "I suppose there is a praise which is rudeness, and that may be mine. At the same time there is a treatment which is injustice, and that may be yours. Because a plain blunt man, who has never been taught concealment, speaks out his mind without exactly intending it, he's to be snapped off like the son of a sinner." "Indeed there's no such case between us." she said, turning away. "I don't allow strangers to be bold and impudent — even in praise of me." "Ah — it is not the fact but the method which offends you." he said, carelessly. "But I have the sad satis- faction of knowing that my words, whether pleasing or offensive, are unmistakably true. Would you have had me look at you, and tell my acquaintance that you are quite a common-place woman, to save you the embar- rassment of being stared at if they come near you?

FAR FROM THE MADDING CROWD
BY THOMAS HARDY, 1874

# Create a poem about Gratitude

"When inviting a lady to dance, if she replies very politely, asking to be excused, as she does not wish to dance ('with you,' being probably her mental reservation), a man ought to be satisfied. At all events, he should never press her to dance after one refusal. The set forms which Turveydrop would give for the invitation are too much of the deportment school to be used in practice. If you know a young lady slightly, it is sufficient to say to her, 'May I have the pleasure of dancing this waltz, &c., with you?' or if intimately, 'Will you dance, Miss A—?' The young lady who has refused one gentleman, has no right to accept another for that dance; and young ladies who do not wish to be annoyed, must take care not to accept two gentlemen for the same dance. In Germany such innocent blunders often cause fatal results. Two partners arrive at the same moment to claim the fair one's hand; she vows{98} she has not made a mistake; 'was sure she was engaged to Herr A—, and not to Herr B—;' Herr B— is equally certain that she was engaged to him. The awkwardness is, that if he at once gives her up, he appears to be indifferent about it; while, if he presses his suit, he must quarrel with Herr A—, unless the damsel is clever enough to satisfy both of them; and particularly if there is an especial interest in Herr B—, he yields at last, but when the dance is over, sends a friend to Herr A—. Absurd as all this is, it is common, and I have often seen one Herr or the other walking about with a huge gash on his cheek, or his arm in a sling, a few days after a ball. "Friendship, it appears, can be let out on hire. The lady who was so very amiable to you last night, has a right to ignore your existence to-day. In fact, a ball room acquaintance rarely goes any farther, until you have met at more balls than one. In the same way a man cannot, after being introduced to a young lady to dance with, ask her to do so more than twice in the same evening. A man may dance four or even five times with the same partner. On the other hand, a real well-bred man will wish to be useful, and there are certain people whom it is imperative on him to ask to dance—the daughters of the house, for instance, and any young ladies whom he may know intimately; but most of all the well-bred and amiable man will sacrifice himself to those plain, ill-dressed, dull looking beings who cling to the wall, unsought and despairing. After all, he will not regret his good nature. The spirits reviving at the unexpected invitation, the wall-flower will{99} pour out her best conversation, will dance her best, and will show him

THE GENTLEMEN'S BOOK OF ETIQUETTE,
AND MANUAL OF POLITENESS;
BY CECIL B. HARTLEY.

# Create a poem your Face

He was the only man of us who still "followed the sea." The worst that could be said of him was that he did not represent his class. He was a seaman, but he was a wanderer, too, while most seamen lead, if one may so express it, a sedentary life. Their minds are of the stay-at-home order, and their home is always with them—the ship; and so is their country—the sea. One ship is very much like another, and the sea is always the same. In the immutability of their surroundings the foreign shores, the foreign faces, the changing immensity of life, glide past, veiled not by a sense of mystery but by a slightly disdainful ignorance; for there is nothing mysterious to a seaman unless it be the sea itself, which is the mistress of his existence and as inscrutable as Destiny. For the rest, after his hours of work, a casual stroll or a casual spree on shore suffices to unfold for him the secret of a whole continent, and generally he finds the secret not worth knowing. The yarns of seamen have a direct simplicity, the whole meaning of which lies within the shell of a cracked nut. But Marlow was not typical (if his propensity to spin yarns be excepted), and to him the meaning of an episode was not inside like a kernel but outside, enveloping the tale which brought it out only as a glow brings out a haze, in the likeness of one of these misty halos that sometimes are made visible by the spectral illumination of moonshine. His remark did not seem at all surprising. It was just like Marlow. It was accepted in silence. No one took the trouble to grunt even; and presently he said, very slow—"I was thinking of very old times, when the Romans first came here, nineteen hundred years ago—the other day .... Light came out of this river since—you say Knights? Yes; but it is like a running blaze on a plain, like a flash of lightning in the clouds. We live in the flicker—may it last as long as the old earth keeps rolling! But darkness was here yesterday. Imagine the feelings of a commander of a fine—what d'ye call 'em?—trireme in the Mediterranean, ordered suddenly to the north; run overland across the Gauls in a hurry; put in charge of one of these craft the legionaries—a wonderful lot of handy men they must have been, too—used to build, apparently by the hundred, in a month or two, if we may believe what we read. Imagine him here—the very end of the world, a sea the colour of lead, a sky the colour of smoke, a kind of ship about as rigid as a concertina—and going up this river with stores, or orders, or what you like. Sand-banks, marshes, forests, savages,—precious little to

HEART OF DARKNESS
BY JOSEPH CONRAD

# Create a poem about Time

After a little while, I set to work to describe the events of the intervening years of my youth, and early middle age; which included most of my gallant intrigues and adventures of a frisky order; but not the more lascivious ones of later years. Then an illness caused me to think seriously of burning the whole. But not liking to destroy my labor, I laid it aside again for a couple of years. Then another illness gave me long uninterrupted leisure; I read my manuscript, and filled in some occurrences which I had forgotten, but which my diary enabled me to place in their proper order. This will account for the difference in style in places, which I now observe; and a very needless repetition, of voluptuous descriptions, which I had forgotten, had been before described; that however is inevitable, for human copulation, vary the incidents leading up to it as you may, is, and must be, at all times, much the same affair. Then for the first time, I thought I would print my work that had been commenced more than twenty years before, but hesitated. I then had entered my maturity, and on to the most lascivious portion of my life, the events were disjointed, and fragmentary and my amusement was to describe them just after they occurred. Most frequently the next day I wrote all down with much prolixity, since, I have much abbreviated it. I had from youth an excellent memory, but about sexual matters a wonderful one. Women were the pleasure of my life. I loved cunt, but also she who had it; I like the woman I fucked and not simply the cunt I fucked, and therein is a great difference. I recollect even now in a degree which astonishes me, the face, color, stature, thighs, backside, and cunt, of well nigh every woman I have had, who was not a mere casual; and even of some who were. The clothes they wore, the houses and rooms in which I had them, were before me mentally, as I wrote, the way the bed, and furniture were placed, the side of the room the windows were on, I remembered perfectly; and all the important events I can fix as to time, sufficiently nearly by reference to my diary, in which the contemporaneous circumstances of my life are recorded. I recollect also largely what we said, and did, and generally our baudy amusements. Where I fail to have done so, I have left description blank, rather than attempt to make a story coherent by inserting what was merely probable. I could not now account for my course of action, nor why I did this, or said that, my conduct seems strange, foolish, absurd, very frequently, that of some

MY SECRET LIFE
BY AN ANONYMOUS AUTHOR

# Create a poem about Rain

I recall many incidents of the summer of 1887 that followed my soul's sudden awakening. I did nothing but explore with my hands and learn the name of every object that I touched; and the more I handled things and learned their names and uses, the more joyous and confident grew my sense of kinship with the rest of the world. When the time of daisies and buttercups came Miss Sullivan took me by the hand across the fields, where men were preparing the earth for the seed, to the banks of the Tennessee River, and there, sitting on the warm grass, I had my first lessons in the beneficence of nature. I learned how the sun and the rain make to grow out of the ground every tree that is pleasant to the sight and good for food, how birds build their nests and live and thrive from land to land, how the squirrel, the deer, the lion and every other creature finds food and shelter. As my knowledge of things grew I felt more and more the delight of the world I was in. Long before I learned to do a sum in arithmetic or describe the shape of the earth, Miss Sullivan had taught me to find beauty in the fragrant woods, in every blade of grass, and in the curves and dimples of my baby sister's hand. She linked my earliest thoughts with nature, and made me feel that "birds and flowers and I were happy peers." But about this time I had an experience which taught me that nature is not always kind. One day my teacher and I were returning from a long ramble. The morning had been fine, but it was growing warm and sultry when at last we turned our faces homeward. Two or three times we stopped to rest under a tree by the wayside. Our last halt was under a wild cherry tree a short distance from the house. The shade was grateful, and the tree was so easy to climb that with my teacher's assistance I was able to scramble to a seat in the branches. It was so cool up in the tree that Miss Sullivan proposed that we have our luncheon there. I promised to keep still while she went to the house to fetch it. Suddenly a change passed over the tree. All the sun's warmth left the air. I knew the sky was black, because all the heat, which meant light to me, had died out of the atmosphere. A strange odour came up from the earth. I knew it, it was the odour that always precedes a thunderstorm, and a nameless fear clutched at my heart. I felt absolutely alone, cut off from my friends and the firm earth. The immense, the unknown, enfolded me. I remained still and expectant; a chilling terror crept over me. I longed for my teacher's return; but above all things I wanted to get down from that tree. There was a moment of

**THE STORY OF MY LIFE
BY HELEN KELLER**

# Create a poem about the color Red

In pursuance of this determination, little Oliver, to his excessive astonishment, was released from bondage, and ordered to put himself into a clean shirt. He had hardly achieved this very unusual gymnastic performance, when Mr. Bumble brought him, with his own hands, a basin of gruel, and the holiday allowance of two ounces and a quarter of bread. At this tremendous sight, Oliver began to cry very piteously: thinking, not unnaturally, that the board must have determined to kill him for some useful purpose, or they never would have begun to fatten him up in that way. 'Don't make your eyes red, Oliver, but eat your food and be thankful,' said Mr. Bumble, in a tone of impressive pomposity. 'You're a going to be made a 'prentice of, Oliver.' 'A prentice, sir!' said the child, trembling. 'Yes, Oliver,' said Mr. Bumble. 'The kind and blessed gentleman which is so many parents to you, Oliver, when you have none of your own: are a going to 'prentice' you: and to set you up in life, and make a man of you: although the expense to the parish is three pound ten!—three pound ten, Oliver!—seventy shillins—one hundred and forty sixpences!—and all for a naughty orphan which nobody can't love.' As Mr. Bumble paused to take breath, after delivering this address in an awful voice, the tears rolled down the poor child's face, and he sobbed bitterly. 'Come,' said Mr. Bumble, somewhat less pompously, for it was gratifying to his feelings to observe the effect his eloquence had produced; 'Come, Oliver! Wipe your eyes with the cuffs of your jacket, and don't cry into your gruel; that's a very foolish action, Oliver.' It certainly was, for there was quite enough water in it already. On their way to the magistrate, Mr. Bumble instructed Oliver that all he would have to do, would be to look very happy, and say, when the gentleman asked him if he wanted to be apprenticed, that he should like it very much indeed; both of which injunctions Oliver promised to obey: the rather as Mr. Bumble threw in a gentle hint, that if he failed in either particular, there was no telling what would be done to him. When they arrived at the office, he was shut up in a little room by himself, and admonished by Mr. Bumble to stay there, until he came back to fetch him. There the boy remained, with a palpitating heart, for half an hour. At the expiration of which time Mr. Bumble thrust in his head, unadorned with the cocked hat, and said aloud: 'Now, Oliver, my dear, come to the gentleman.' As Mr. Bumble said this, he put on a grim and threatening look, and added, in a low voice, 'Mind what I told you, you young rascal!'

OLIVER TWIST OR THE PARISH BOY'S PROGRESS
BY CHARLES DICKENS

# Create a poem about Writing

If you wish to charge a fee or distribute a Project Gutenberg-tm electronic work or group of works on different terms than are set forth in this agreement, you must obtain permission in writing from both the Project Gutenberg Literary Archive Foundation and Michael Hart, the owner of the Project Gutenberg-tm trademark. Contact the Foundation as set forth in Section 3 below. 1.F.1. Project Gutenberg volunteers and employees expend considerable effort to identify, do copyright research on, transcribe and proofread public domain works in creating the Project Gutenberg-tm collection. Despite these efforts, Project Gutenberg-tm electronic works, and the medium on which they may be stored, may contain "Defects," such as, but not limited to, incomplete, inaccurate or corrupt data, transcription errors, a copyright or other intellectual property infringement, a defective or damaged disk or other medium, a computer virus, or computer codes that damage or cannot be read by your equipment. LIMITED WARRANTY, DISCLAIMER OF DAMAGES - Except for the "Right of Replacement or Refund" described in paragraph 1.F.3, the Project Gutenberg Literary Archive Foundation, the owner of the Project Gutenberg-tm trademark, and any other party distributing a Project Gutenberg-tm electronic work under this agreement, disclaim all liability to you for damages, costs and expenses, including legal fees. YOU AGREE THAT YOU HAVE NO REMEDIES FOR NEGLIGENCE, STRICT LIABILITY, BREACH OF WARRANTY OR BREACH OF CONTRACT EXCEPT THOSE PROVIDED IN PARAGRAPH F3. YOU AGREE THAT THE FOUNDATION, THE TRADEMARK OWNER, AND ANY DISTRIBUTOR UNDER THIS AGREEMENT WILL NOT BE LIABLE TO YOU FOR ACTUAL, DIRECT, INDIRECT, CONSEQUENTIAL, PUNITIVE OR INCIDENTAL DAMAGES EVEN IF YOU GIVE NOTICE OF THE POSSIBILITY OF SUCH DAMAGE. LIMITED RIGHT OF REPLACEMENT OR REFUND - If you discover a defect in this electronic work within 90 days of receiving it, you can receive a refund of the money (if any) you paid for it by sending a written explanation to the person you received the work from. If you received the work on a physical medium, you must return the medium with your written explanation. The person or entity that provided you with the defective work may elect to provide a replacement copy in lieu of a refund. If you received the work electronically, the person or entity providing it to you may choose to give you a second opportunity to receive the work electronically in lieu of a refund. If the second copy is also defective, you may demand

A MODEST PROPOSAL
BY DR. JONATHAN SWIFT

# Create a poem about Dogs

He lifted the jeep and started off; the lorry, and the scows and the other lorry, followed; the snooper and the bomb-robots went ahead like a pack of hunting dogs. They went through great chambers, dark and silent and bulking with dusty machines. Jacquemont explained that the prisoners had never gotten into this section; the Harriet Barne was a mile or so to their right. Conn turned left, when the noise of firing from outside became plainer. A foundry. A machine-shop which seemed to have been abandoned in the middle of some rush job that hadn't really been necessary. They came to a place even the snooper couldn't enter, choked to the ceiling with dead vegetation, hydroponic seed-plants that had been left untended to grow wild and die. They emerged into outside light, in vast caves a mile high and open onto the crater, and looked across the floor that had been leveled and vitrified to the other side, three and a half miles away. He didn't know whether to be more awed by the original eruption that had formed the crater or by the engineering feat of carving these docks and ship-berths, big enough for the hugest hyperspaceship, into it. At first, he had been afraid of getting into position too soon before the task force from outside could profit by the diversion. Then he began to worry about the time it was taking to get halfway around the crater. He could hear artillery thundering continuously above. Except at the very beginning of the battle, there had been little gunfire. He wondered if both sides were running out of lift-and-drive missiles, or if the fighting had gotten too close for anybody to risk using nuclear weapons. He was also worrying about the women and children among the released prisoners. "Why did the pirates bother with them?" he asked Sylvie. "They used the women and some of the old men to do[Pg 86] housekeeping chores for them," she said. "Mostly, though, they were hostages; if the men didn't work, Perales threatened to punish the women and children. I wasn't doing any housework; I'm too good a mechanic. I was helping on the ship." "Well, what'll I do with them when the fighting starts? I can't take them into battle." "You'll have to; it'll be the safest place for them. You can't leave them anywhere and risk having them recaptured." "That means we'll have to detach some men to cover them, and that'll cut our striking force down." He whistled at the sound-pickup of his screen and told his father about it. "What do I do with these people, anyhow?" "You're the officer in command, Conn," his father told him. "Your decision. How soon can you attack? We're

THE COSMIC COMPUTER
BY H. BEAM PIPER

# Create a poem about Cats

I climbed the three dilapidated flights of stairs, which I had so often climbed before, and knocked at a small door at the end of the corridor. Mr. Wilde opened the door and I walked in. When he had double-locked the door and pushed a heavy chest against it, he came and sat down beside me, peering up into my face with his little light-coloured eyes. Half a dozen new scratches covered his nose and cheeks, and the silver wires which supported his artificial ears had become displaced. I thought I had never seen him so hideously fascinating. He had no ears. The artificial ones, which now stood out at an angle from the fine wire, were his one weakness. They were made of wax and painted a shell pink, but the rest of his face was yellow. He might better have revelled in the luxury of some artificial fingers for his left hand, which was absolutely fingerless, but it seemed to cause him no inconvenience, and he was satisfied with his wax ears. He was very small, scarcely higher than a child of ten, but his arms were magnificently developed, and his thighs as thick as any athlete's. Still, the most remarkable thing about Mr. Wilde was that a man of his marvellous intelligence and knowledge should have such a head. It was flat and pointed, like the heads of many of those unfortunates whom people imprison in asylums for the weak-minded. Many called him insane, but I knew him to be as sane as I was. I do not deny that he was eccentric; the mania he had for keeping that cat and teasing her until she flew at his face like a demon, was certainly eccentric. I never could understand why he kept the creature, nor what pleasure he found in shutting himself up in his room with this surly, vicious beast. I remember once, glancing up from the manuscript I was studying by the light of some tallow dips, and seeing Mr. Wilde squatting motionless on his high chair, his eyes fairly blazing with excitement, while the cat, which had risen from her place before the stove, came creeping across the floor right at him. Before I could move she flattened her belly to the ground, crouched, trembled, and sprang into his face. Howling and foaming they rolled over and over on the floor, scratching and clawing, until the cat screamed and fled under the cabinet, and Mr. Wilde turned over on his back, his limbs contracting and curling up like the legs of a dying spider. He was eccentric. Mr. Wilde had climbed into his high chair, and, after studying my face, picked up a dog's-eared ledger and opened it. "Henry B. Matthews," he read, "book-keeper with Whysot Whysot and Company, dealers in church

THE KING IN YELLOW
BY ROBERT W. CHAMBERS

# Create a poem about Farewells

Not because they are afraid, but because, as Ts`ao Kung says, "all have embraced the firm resolution to do or die." We may remember that the heroes of the Iliad were equally childlike in showing their emotion. Chang Yu alludes to the mournful parting at the I River between Ching K`o and his friends, when the former was sent to attempt the life of the King of Ch`in (afterwards First Emperor) in 227 B.C. The tears of all flowed down like rain as he bade them farewell and uttered the following lines: "The shrill blast is blowing, Chilly the burn; Your champion is going—Not to return." But let them once be brought to bay, and they will display the courage of a Chu or a Kuei. Chu was the personal name of Chuan Chu, a native of the Wu State and contemporary with Sun Tzu himself, who was employed by Kung-tzu Kuang, better known as Ho Lu Wang, to assassinate his sovereign Wang Liao with a dagger which he secreted in the belly of a fish served up at a banquet. He succeeded in his attempt, but was immediately hacked to pieced by the king's bodyguard. This was in 515 B.C. The other hero referred to, Ts`ao Kuei (or Ts`ao Mo), performed the exploit which has made his name famous 166 years earlier, in 681 B.C. Lu had been thrice defeated by Ch`i, and was just about to conclude a treaty surrendering a large slice of territory, when Ts`ao Kuei suddenly seized Huan Kung, the Duke of Ch`i, as he stood on the altar steps and held a dagger against his chest. None of the duke's retainers dared to move a muscle, and Ts`ao Kuei proceeded to demand full restitution, declaring the Lu was being unjustly treated because she was a smaller and a weaker state. Huan Kung, in peril of his life, was obliged to consent, whereupon Ts`ao Kuei flung away his dagger and quietly resumed his place amid the terrified assemblage without having so much as changed color. As was to be expected, the Duke wanted afterwards to repudiate the bargain, but his wise old counselor Kuan Chung pointed out to him the impolicy of breaking his word, and the upshot was that this bold stroke regained for Lu the whole of what she had lost in three pitched battles.] 29. The skillful tactician may be likened to the SHUAI-JAN. Now the SHUAI-JAN is a snake that is found in the Ch`ang mountains. ["Shuai-jan" means "suddenly" or "rapidly," and the snake in question was doubtless so called owing to the rapidity of its movements. Through this passage, the term in the Chinese has now come to be used in the sense of "military maneuvers."] Strike at its head, and you will be attacked by its tail; strike at its tail, and you will be attacked by its

SUN TZU ON THE ART OF WAR
BY LIONEL GILES, M.A.

# Create a poem about Dreams

Ham Peggotty, who went to the national school, and was a very dragon at his catechism, and who may therefore be regarded as a credible witness, reported next day, that happening to peep in at the parlour-door an hour after this, he was instantly descried by Miss Betsey, then walking to and fro in a state of agitation, and pounced upon before he could make his escape. That there were now occasional sounds of feet and voices overhead which he inferred the cotton did not exclude, from the circumstance of his evidently being clutched by the lady as a victim on whom to expend her superabundant agitation when the sounds were loudest. That, marching him constantly up and down by the collar (as if he had been taking too much laudanum), she, at those times, shook him, rumpled his hair, made light of his linen, stopped his ears as if she confounded them with her own, and otherwise tousled and maltreated him. This was in part confirmed by his aunt, who saw him at half past twelve o'clock, soon after his release, and affirmed that he was then as red as I was  The mild Mr. Chillip could not possibly bear malice at such a time, if at any time. He sidled into the parlour as soon as he was at liberty, and said to my aunt in his meekest manner: 'Well, ma'am, I am happy to congratulate you.' 'What upon?' said my aunt, sharply. Mr. Chillip was fluttered again, by the extreme severity of my aunt's manner; so he made her a little bow and gave her a little smile, to mollify her. Mercy on the man, what's he doing!' cried my aunt, impatiently. 'Can't he speak?' 'Be calm, my dear ma'am,' said Mr. Chillip, in his softest accents. 'There is no longer any occasion for uneasiness, ma'am. Be calm.' It has since been considered almost a miracle that my aunt didn't shake him, and shake what he had to say, out of him. She only shook her own head at him, but in a way that made him quail. 'Well, ma'am,' resumed Mr. Chillip, as soon as he had courage, 'I am happy to congratulate you. All is now over, ma'am, and well over.' During the five minutes or so that Mr. Chillip devoted to the delivery of this oration, my aunt eyed him narrowly. 'How is she?' said my aunt, folding her arms with her bonnet still tied on one of them. 'Well, ma'am, she will soon be quite comfortable, I hope,' returned Mr. Chillip. 'Quite as comfortable as we can expect a young mother to be, under these melancholy domestic circumstances. There cannot be any objection to your seeing her presently, ma'am. It may do her good.' 'And SHE. How is SHE?' said my aunt, sharply. Mr. Chillip laid his head a little more on one side, and looked at my aunt like an

DAVID COPPERFIELD
BY CHARLES DICKENS

# Create a poem about Hate

"'Tis not much, your Majesty, yet perchance it may beguile a short half-hour for want of a better. My father, Sir Richard, is very rich, and of a most generous nature. My mother died whilst I was yet a boy. I have two brothers: Arthur, my elder, with a soul like to his father's; and Hugh, younger than I, a mean spirit, covetous, treacherous, vicious, underhanded—a reptile. Such was he from the cradle; such was he ten years past, when I last saw him—a ripe rascal at nineteen, I being twenty then, and Arthur twenty-two. There is none other of us but the Lady Edith, my cousin—she was sixteen then—beautiful, gentle, good, the daughter of an earl, the last of her race, heiress of a great fortune and a lapsed title. My father was her guardian. I loved her and she loved me; but she was betrothed to Arthur from the cradle, and Sir Richard would not suffer the contract to be broken. Arthur loved another maid, and bade us be of good cheer and hold fast to the hope that delay and luck together would some day give success to our several causes. Hugh loved the Lady Edith's fortune, though in truth he said it was herself he loved—but then 'twas his way, alway, to say the one thing and mean the other. But he lost his arts upon the girl; he could deceive my father, but none else. My father loved him best of us all, and trusted and believed him; for he was the youngest child, and others hated him—these qualities being in all ages sufficient to win a parent's dearest love; and he had a smooth persuasive tongue, with an admirable gift of lying—and these be qualities which do mightily assist a blind affection to cozen itself. I was wild—in troth I might go yet farther and say very wild, though 'twas a wildness of an innocent sort, since it hurt none but me, brought shame to none, nor loss, nor had in it any taint of crime or baseness, or what might not beseem mine honourable degree. "Yet did my brother Hugh turn these faults to good account—he seeing that our brother Arthur's health was but indifferent, and hoping the worst might work him profit were I swept out of the path—so—but 'twere a long tale, good my liege, and little worth the telling. Briefly, then, this brother did deftly magnify my faults and make them crimes; ending his base work with finding a silken ladder in mine apartments—conveyed thither by his own means—and did convince my father by this, and suborned evidence of servants and other lying knaves, that I was minded to carry off my Edith and marry with her in rank defiance of his will. "Three years of banishment from home

THE PRINCE AND THE PAUPER
BY MARK TWAIN

# Create a poem about Hope

Dinocrates, an architect who was full of confidence in his own ideas and skill, set out from Macedonia, in the reign of Alexander, to go to the army, being eager to win the approbation of the king. He took with him from his country letters from relatives and friends to the principal military men and officers of the court, in order to gain access to them more readily. Being politely received by them, he asked to be presented to Alexander as soon as possible. They promised, but were rather slow, waiting for a suitable opportunity. So Dinocrates, thinking that they were playing with him, had recourse to his own efforts. He was of very lofty stature and pleasing countenance, finely formed, and extremely dignified. Trusting, therefore, to these natural gifts, he undressed himself in his inn, anointed his body with oil, set a chaplet of poplar leaves on his head, draped his left shoulder with a lion's skin, and holding a club in his right hand stalked forth to a place in front of the tribunal where the king was administering justice. 2. His strange appearance made the people turn round, and this led Alexander to look at him. In astonishment he gave orders to make way for him to draw near, and asked who he was. "Dinocrates," quoth he, "a Macedonian architect, who brings thee ideas and designs worthy of thy renown. I have made a design for the shaping of Mount Athos into the statue of a man, in whose left hand I have represented a very spacious fortified city, and in his right a bowl to receive the water of all the streams which are in that mountain, so that it may pour from the bowl into the sea." 3. Alexander, delighted with the idea of his design, immediately inquired whether there were any fields in the neighbourhood[36] that could maintain the city in corn. On finding that this was impossible without transport from beyond the sea, "Dinocrates," quoth he, "I appreciate your design as excellent in composition, and I am delighted with it, but I apprehend that anybody who should found a city in that spot would be censured for bad judgement. For as a newborn babe cannot be nourished without the nurse's milk, nor conducted to the approaches that lead to growth in life, so a city cannot thrive without fields and the fruits thereof pouring into its walls, nor have a large population without plenty of food, nor maintain its population without a supply of it. Therefore, while thinking that your design is commendable, I consider the site as not commendable; but I would have you stay with me, because I mean to make use of your services." 4. From that

VITRUVIUS THE TEN BOOKS ON ARCHITECTURE
BY MORRIS HICKY MORGAN, PH.D., LL.D.

# Create a poem about Imagination

However, the government does not concern me much, and I shall bestow the fewest possible thoughts on it. It is not many moments that I live under a government, even in this world. If a man is thought-free, fancy-free, imagination-free, that which is not never for a long time appearing to be to him, unwise rulers or reformers cannot fatally interrupt him. I know that most men think differently from myself; but those whose lives are by profession devoted to the study of these or kindred subjects, content me as little as any. Statesmen and legislators, standing so completely within the institution, never distinctly and nakedly behold it. They speak of moving society, but have no resting-place without it. They may be men of a certain experience and discrimination, and have no doubt invented ingenious and even useful systems, for which we sincerely thank them; but all their wit and usefulness lie within certain not very wide limits. They are wont to forget that the world is not governed by policy and expediency. Webster never goes behind government, and so cannot speak with authority about it. His words are wisdom to those legislators who contemplate no essential reform in the existing government; but for thinkers, and those who legislate for all time, he never once glances at the subject. I know of those whose serene and wise speculations on this theme would soon reveal the limits of his mind's range and hospitality. Yet, compared with the cheap professions of most reformers, and the still cheaper wisdom and eloquence of politicians in general, his are almost the only sensible and valuable words, and we thank Heaven for him. Comparatively, he is always strong, original, and, above all, practical. Still, his quality is not wisdom, but prudence. The lawyer's truth is not truth, but consistency or a consistent expediency. Truth is always in harmony with herself, and is not concerned chiefly to reveal the justice that may consist with wrong-doing. He well deserves to be called, as he has been called, the Defender of the Constitution. There are really no blows to be given by him but defensive ones. He is not a leader, but a follower. His leaders are the men of '87. "I have never made an effort," he says, "and never propose to make an effort; I have never countenanced an effort, and never mean to countenance an effort, to disturb the arrangement as originally made, by which the various States came into the Union." Still thinking of the sanction which the Constitution gives to slavery, he says, "Because it was a part of the original

WALDEN, AND ON THE DUTY OF
CIVIL DISOBEDIENCE
BY HENRY DAVID THOREAU

# Create a poem about Jealousy

I could see as he looked down that he was repressing some internal emotion. His features were still composed, but his eyes shone with amused exultation. "Excuse the admiration of a connoisseur," said he as he waved his hand towards the line of portraits which covered the opposite wall. "Watson won't allow that I know anything of art but that is mere jealousy because our views upon the subject differ. Now, these are a really very fine series of portraits." "Well, I'm glad to hear you say so," said Sir Henry, glancing with some surprise at my friend. "I don't pretend to know much about these things, and I'd be a better judge of a horse or a steer than of a picture. I didn't know that you found time for such things." "I know what is good when I see it, and I see it now. That's a Kneller, I'll swear, that lady in the blue silk over yonder, and the stout gentleman with the wig ought to be a Reynolds. They are all family portraits, I presume?" "Every one." "Do you know the names?" "Barrymore has been coaching me in them, and I think I can say my lessons fairly well." "Who is the gentleman with the telescope?" "That is Rear-Admiral Baskerville, who served under Rodney in the West Indies. The man with the blue coat and the roll of paper is Sir William Baskerville, who was Chairman of Committees of the House of Commons under Pitt." "And this Cavalier opposite to me—the one with the black velvet and the lace?" "Ah, you have a right to know about him. That is the cause of all the mischief, the wicked Hugo, who started the Hound of the Baskervilles. We're not likely to forget him." I gazed with interest and some surprise upon the portrait. "Dear me!" said Holmes, "he seems a quiet, meek-mannered man enough, but I dare say that there was a lurking devil in his eyes. I had pictured him as a more robust and ruffianly person." "There's no doubt about the authenticity, for the name and the date, 1647, are on the back of the canvas." Holmes said little more, but the picture of the old roysterer seemed to have a fascination for him, and his eyes were continually fixed upon it during supper. It was not until later, when Sir Henry had gone to his room, that I was able to follow the trend of his thoughts. He led me back into the banqueting-hall, his bedroom candle in his hand, and he held it up against the time-stained portrait on the wall. "Do you see anything there?" I looked at the broad plumed hat, the curling love-locks, the white lace collar, and the straight, severe face which was framed between them. It was not a brutal countenance, but it was prim, hard, and stern, with a firm-set, thin-lipped mouth,

# THE HOUND OF THE BASKERVILLES
## BY A. CONAN DOYLE

# Create a poem about Winter

Anna Pavlovna's drawing room was gradually filling. The highest Petersburg society was assembled there: people differing widely in age and character but alike in the social circle to which they belonged. Prince Vasili's daughter, the beautiful Helene, came to take her father to the ambassador's entertainment; she wore a ball dress and her badge as maid of honor. The youthful little Princess Bolkonskaya, known as la femme la plus seduisante de Petersbourg, * was also there. She had been married during the previous winter, and being pregnant did not go to any large gatherings, but only to small receptions. Prince Vasili's son, Hippolyte, had come with Mortemart, whom he introduced. The Abbe Morio and many others had also come. To each new arrival Anna Pavlovna said, "You have not yet seen my aunt," or "You do not know my aunt?" and very gravely conducted him or her to a little old lady, wearing large bows of ribbon in her cap, who had come sailing in from another room as soon as the guests began to arrive; and slowly turning her eyes from the visitor to her aunt, Anna Pavlovna mentioned each one's name and then left them. Each visitor performed the ceremony of greeting this old aunt whom not one of them knew, not one of them wanted to know, and not one of them cared about; Anna Pavlovna observed these greetings with mournful and solemn interest and silent approval. The aunt spoke to each of them in the same words, about their health and her own, and the health of Her Majesty, "who, thank God, was better today." And each visitor, though politeness prevented his showing impatience, left the old woman with a sense of relief at having performed a vexatious duty and did not return to her the whole evening. The young Princess Bolkonskaya had brought some work in a gold-embroidered velvet bag. Her pretty little upper lip, on which a delicate dark down was just perceptible, was too short for her teeth, but it lifted all the more sweetly, and was especially charming when she occasionally drew it down to meet the lower lip. As is always the case with a thoroughly attractive woman, her defect—the shortness of her upper lip and her half-open mouth—seemed to be her own special and peculiar form of beauty. Everyone brightened at the sight of this pretty young woman, so soon to become a mother, so full of life and health, and carrying her burden so lightly. Old men and dull dispirited young ones who looked at her, after being in her company and talking to her a little while, felt as if they too were becoming, like her, full of life and health.

WAR AND PEACE
BY LEO TOLSTOY/TOLSTOI

# Create a poem about Summer

The girls—who indeed are not to take the field—are educated out of the same books as are prepared for the military training of the boys, and so in the female youth arises the same conception which exhausts itself in envy that they have nothing to do with war and in admiration for the military class. What pictures of horror out of all the battles on earth, from the Biblical and Macedonian and Punic Wars down to the Thirty Years' War and the wars of Napoleon, were brought before us tender maidens, who in all other things were formed to be gentle and mild; how we saw there cities burnt and the inhabitants put to the sword and the conquered trodden down—and all this was a real enjoyment; and of course through this heaping up and repetition of the horrors the perception that they were horrors becomes blunted, everything which belongs to the category of war comes no longer to be regarded from the point of view of humanity, and receives a perfectly peculiar mystico-historico-political consecration. War must be—it is the source of the highest dignities and honours—that the girls see very well, and they have had also to learn by heart the poems and tirades in which war is magnified. And thus originate the Spartan mothers, and the "mothers of the colours," and the frequent invitations to the cotillon which are given to a corps of officers when it is the turn of the ladies{5} to choose partners.[1] I was not like so many of my companions in rank educated in a convent, but under the direction of governesses and masters in my father's house. My mother I lost early. Our aunt, an old canoness, filled the place of a mother to us children—for there were three younger children. We spent the winter months in Vienna, the summer on a family estate in Lower Austria. I can remember that I gave my governesses and masters much satisfaction, for I was an industrious and ambitious scholar, gifted with an accurate memory. When I could not, as I have remarked, satisfy my ambition by winning battles like a heroine, I contented myself with passing judgments on them in my lessons, and extorting admiration by my zeal for learning. In the French and English languages I was nearly perfect. In geology and astronomy I made as much progress as was ordinarily accessible in the programme of the education of a girl, but in the subject of history I learned more than was required of me. Out of the library of my father I fetched the ponderous works of history, in which I studied in my leisure hours. I always thought myself a little bit cleverer when I

LAY DOWN YOUR ARMS
BY BERTHA VON SUTTNER

# Create a poem about Smiling

The Time Traveller smiled round at us. Then, still smiling faintly, and with his hands deep in his trousers pockets, he walked slowly out of the room, and we heard his slippers shuffling down the long passage to his laboratory. The Psychologist looked at us. 'I wonder what he's got?' 'Some sleight-of-hand trick or other,' said the Medical Man, and Filby tried to tell us about a conjurer he had seen at Burslem; but before he had finished his preface the Time Traveller came back, and Filby's anecdote collapsed. The thing the Time Traveller held in his hand was a glittering metallic framework, scarcely larger than a small clock, and very delicately made. There was ivory in it, and some transparent crystalline substance. And now I must be explicit, for this that follows—unless his explanation is to be accepted—is an absolutely unaccountable thing. He took one of the small octagonal tables that were scattered about the room, and set it in front of the fire, with two legs on the hearthrug. On this table he placed the mechanism. Then he drew up a chair, and sat down. The only other object on the table was a small shaded lamp, the bright light of which fell upon the model. There were also perhaps a dozen candles about, two in brass candlesticks upon the mantel and several in sconces, so that the room was brilliantly illuminated. I sat in a low arm-chair nearest the fire, and I drew this forward so as to be almost between the Time Traveller and the fireplace. Filby sat behind him, looking over his shoulder. The Medical Man and the Provincial Mayor watched him in profile from the right, the Psychologist from the left. The Very Young Man stood behind the Psychologist. We were all on the alert. It appears incredible to me that any kind of trick, however subtly conceived and however adroitly done, could have been played upon us under these conditions. The Time Traveller looked at us, and then at the mechanism. 'Well?' said the Psychologist. 'This little affair,' said the Time Traveller, resting his elbows upon the table and pressing his hands together above the apparatus, 'is only a model. It is my plan for a machine to travel through time. You will notice that it looks singularly askew, and that there is an odd twinkling appearance about this bar, as though it was in some way unreal.' He pointed to the part with his finger. 'Also, here is one little white lever, and here is another.' The Medical Man got up out of his chair and peered into the thing. 'It's beautifully made,' he said. 'It took two years to make,' retorted the Time Traveller. Then, when we had all

# THE TIME MACHINE
## BY H. G. WELLS [1898]

# Create a poem the Sky

The Dashwoods were now settled at Barton with tolerable comfort to themselves. The house and the garden, with all the objects surrounding them, were now become familiar, and the ordinary pursuits which had given to Norland half its charms were engaged in again with far greater enjoyment than Norland had been able to afford, since the loss of their father. Sir John Middleton, who called on them every day for the first fortnight, and who was not in the habit of seeing much occupation at home, could not conceal his amazement on finding them always employed. Their visitors, except those from Barton Park, were not many; for, in spite of Sir John's urgent entreaties that they would mix more in the neighbourhood, and repeated assurances of his carriage being always at their service, the independence of Mrs. Dashwood's spirit overcame the wish of society for her children; and she was resolute in declining to visit any family beyond the distance of a walk. There were but few who could be so classed; and it was not all of them that were attainable. About a mile and a half from the cottage, along the narrow winding valley of Allenham, which issued from that of Barton, as formerly described, the girls had, in one of their earliest walks, discovered an ancient respectable looking mansion which, by reminding them a little of Norland, interested their imagination and made them wish to be better acquainted with it. But they learnt, on enquiry, that its possessor, an elderly lady of very good character, was unfortunately too infirm to mix with the world, and never stirred from home. The whole country about them abounded in beautiful walks. The high downs which invited them from almost every window of the cottage to seek the exquisite enjoyment of air on their summits, were a happy alternative when the dirt of the valleys beneath shut up their superior beauties; and towards one of these hills did Marianne and Margaret one memorable morning direct their steps, attracted by the partial sunshine of a showery sky, and unable longer to bear the confinement which the settled rain of the two preceding days had occasioned. The weather was not tempting enough to draw the two others from their pencil and their book, in spite of Marianne's declaration that the day would be lastingly fair, and that every threatening cloud would be drawn off from their hills; and the two girls set off together. They gaily ascended the downs, rejoicing in their own penetration at every glimpse of blue sky; and when they caught in their faces the animating gales of a high

SENSE AND SENSIBILITY
BY JANE AUSTEN

# Create a poem about the Ocean

Prince Trask of Tanith and Prince Simon Bentrik were dining together on an upper terrace of what had originally been the mansion house of a Federation period plantation. It had been a number of other things since; now it was the municipal building of a town that had grown around it, which had, somehow, escaped undamaged from the Dunnan blitz. Normally about five or ten thousand, the place was now jammed with almost fifty thousand homeless refugees from half a dozen other towns that had been destroyed, overflowing the buildings and crowding into a sprawling camp of hastily built huts and shelters, and already permanent buildings were going up to accommodate them. Everybody, locals, Mardukans and Space Vikings, had been busy with the work of relief and reconstruction; this was the first meal the two commanders had been able to share in any leisure at all. Prince Bentrik's enjoyment of it was somewhat impaired by the fact that from where he sat he could see, in the distance, the sphere of his disabled ship. "I doubt we can get her off-planet again, let alone into hyperspace." "Well, we'll get you and your crew to Marduk in the Nemesis, then." They were both speaking loudly, above the clank and clatter of machinery below. "I hope you didn't think I'd leave you stranded here." "I don't know how either of us will be received. Space Vikings haven't been exactly popular on Marduk, lately. They may thank you for bringing me back to stand trial," Bentrik said bitterly. "Why, I'd have anybody shot who let his ship get caught as I did mine. Those two were down in atmosphere before I knew they'd come out of hyperspace." "I think they were down on the planet before your ship arrived." "Oh, that's ridiculous, Prince Trask!" the Mardukan cried. "You can't hide a ship on a planet. Not from the kind of instruments we have in the Royal Navy." "We have pretty fair detection ourselves," Trask reminded him. "There's one place where you can do it. At the bottom of an ocean, with a thousand or so feet of water over her. That's where I was going to hide the Nemesis, if I got here ahead of Dunnan." Prince Bentrik's fork stopped half way to his mouth. He lowered it slowly to his plate. That was a theory he'd like to accept, if he could. "But the locals. They didn't know about it." "They wouldn't. They have no off-planet detection of their own. Come in directly over the ocean, out of the sun, and nobody'd see the ship." "Is that a regular Space Viking trick?" "No. I invented it myself, on the way from Seshat. But if Dunnan wanted to ambush your ship, he'd have thought of it, too. It's the only

SPACE VIKING
BY H. BEAM PIPER

# Create a poem about Art

Mr. Phileas Fogg lived, in 1872, at No. 7, Saville Row, Burlington Gardens, the house in which Sheridan died in 1814. He was one of the most noticeable members of the Reform Club, though he seemed always to avoid attracting attention; an enigmatical personage, about whom little was known, except that he was a polished man of the world. People said that he resembled Byron—at least that his head was Byronic; but he was a bearded, tranquil Byron, who might live on a thousand years without growing old. Certainly an Englishman, it was more doubtful whether Phileas Fogg was a Londoner. He was never seen on 'Change, nor at the Bank, nor in the counting-rooms of the "City"; no ships ever came into London docks of which he was the owner; he had no public employment; he had never been entered at any of the Inns of Court, either at the Temple, or Lincoln's Inn, or Gray's Inn; nor had his voice ever resounded in the Court of Chancery, or in the Exchequer, or the Queen's Bench, or the Ecclesiastical Courts. He certainly was not a manufacturer; nor was he a merchant or a gentleman farmer. His name was strange to the scientific and learned societies, and he never was known to take part in the sage deliberations of the Royal Institution or the London Institution, the Artisan's Association, or the Institution of Arts and Sciences. He belonged, in fact, to none of the numerous societies which swarm in the English capital, from the Harmonic to that of the Entomologists, founded mainly for the purpose of abolishing pernicious insects. Phileas Fogg was a member of the Reform, and that was all. The way in which he got admission to this exclusive club was simple enough. He was recommended by the Barings, with whom he had an open credit. His cheques were regularly paid at sight from his account current, which was always flush. Was Phileas Fogg rich? Undoubtedly. But those who knew him best could not imagine how he had made his fortune, and Mr. Fogg was the last person to whom to apply for the information. He was not lavish, nor, on the contrary, avaricious; for, whenever he knew that money was needed for a noble, useful, or benevolent purpose, he supplied it quietly and sometimes anonymously. He was, in short, the least communicative of men. He talked very little, and seemed all the more mysterious for his taciturn manner. His daily habits were quite open to observation; but whatever he did was so exactly the same thing that he had always done before, that the wits of the curious were fairly puzzled. Had he travelled? It was likely, for no one seemed

AROUND THE WORLD IN EIGHTY DAYS
BY JULES VERNE

Made in United States
Cleveland, OH
27 December 2024